THE EUCHARIST
IN THÉODORE DE BÈZE
AND ST. FRANCIS DE SALES

Saint François de Sales catéchisant Théodore de Bèze.
Gravure d'Elmerich, d'après le tableau de Gamen-Dupasquier.

THE EUCHARIST
IN THÉODORE DE BÈZE
AND ST. FRANCIS DE SALES

William C. Marceau

Toronto Studies in Theology
Volume 59

The Edwin Mellen Press
Lewiston/Queenston/Lampeter

8V
823
.M364
1993

Library of Congress Cataloging-in-Publication Data

This volume has been registered with The Library of Congress.

This is volume 59 in the continuing series
Toronto Studies in Theology
Volume 59 ISBN 0-7734-9693-9
TST Series ISBN 0-88946-975-X

A CIP catalog record for this book
is available from the British Library.

Copyright ©1993 The Edwin Mellen Press

The Edwin Mellen Press   The Edwin Mellen Press
        Box 450   Box 67
   Lewiston, New York   Queenston, Ontario
      USA 14092   CANADA L0S 1L0

Edwin Mellen Press, Ltd.
Lampeter, Dyfed, Wales
UNITED KINGDOM SA48 7DY

Printed in the United States of America

Dedicated to the
Members of
The Congregation of St. Basil

TABLE OF CONTENTS

List of Illustrations

INTRODUCTION

Man reveals himself in his relationships with people. Both Théodore de Bèze and St. Francis de Sales manifested themselves in their relations with each other and with their respective communities. Ideas provoke persons to interact when they are in society. We should like to understand the two subjects of this study by considering an idea that was held by both of them: namely, the Eucharist. This is a means of observing them act on the basis of a concept which was different according to the beliefs of each individual. Théodore de Bèze, the direct successor of Calvin, and Francis de Sales were historical contemporaries, though the former was older. Each inherited his notion of the Eucharist from his predecessors: de Bèze from Calvin and Francis from a consensus of Catholic theologians and the doctrines of the Council of Trent.

We propose, therefore, to better know each of these famous figures through the thought of which they are tributary. De Bèze was an extremely faithful follower and friend to his mentor, John Calvin. It is impossible to neglect the ultra-important work of Calvin in those which became the doctrinal foundations of the teachings of his successor. However, it is equally important to realize that he applied his own genius in subsequently presenting these Calvinistic teachings. Equally paramount is that work of the predecessors of Francis de Sales in his apostolate as priest, missionary and finally bishop. When he announces in the preface to *The Introduction to the Devout Life* that he will simply dispose the variety of flowers in his bouquet as did Glycera, he means that he will collect the individual notions from everywhere in the garden of the Roman Church. With these blossoms from the Bible and from the Church Fathers, both ancient and contemporary, would he form his teachings that would win him ultimately the title of "Doctor of the Church." One of the major faith-convictions that will motivate each of these leaders will be that of the Eucharist.

In an effort then to understand the doctrinal content of the Eucharist in each of these individuals so faithful to his own tradition, we shall examine first the teachings of John Calvin that were given to Théodore de Bèze from the great Reformer himself. Their respective importance in the history of the Reformation itself is commemorated in the stone carvings of that wonderful wall opposite the entrance of the University of Geneva. Next to each other they stand, proposing to the world their means of purifying that doctrine and practice of the mother of all Christian churches. The comparable effigy is in the city where Francis de Sales exercised the bishopric of Geneva: namely, Annecy. The monuments serve to remind all passers of the importance of the lives of each of these men.

Théodore de Bèze strove valiantly to transmit the teaching of Calvin in his doctrine of the "sainte Cène." For this reason, we shall approach de Bèze in our first chapter through a study of his friend's very well composed *Le petit traité sur la sainte Cène*. A rather detailed study of this writing will give us a solid, fundamental grasp of the Reformers' initial ideas of this important doctrine of the Eucharist. Only with this relatively elementary understanding can we hope to appreciate the work of de Bèze in this sacramental area.

To know the doctrines of both men is essential to this study. If we do not observe them in their likenesses and in their differences, we shall not arrive at an integral understanding of their convictions. With this in mind, we shall proceed in a second chapter to investigate the Eucharist teaching of Francis de Sales. His approach is understandably quite different from that of de Bèze. He is a very active priest, missionary and bishop when he writes these ideas which treat of the sacrament. Both men, being Renaissance humanists, had their own particular manners of presenting the Eucharist doctrine. The content and the form of this redaction is distinctively of the

French Renaissance. It is for this reason that we present the texts in the French in which they were written in the 16th and 17th centuries. Not to do so would be to ignore the knowledge and convictions of our two authors as well as to minimize the genius of each in his oratorical and writing abilities within the distinct historical setting proper to the two men.

Having partially analyzed the doctrinal finesse of each of our subjects, we shall seek to establish the historical setting in which each of them taught his doctrine. Our third chapter will bring out some of the characteristics in the France of the Regency: that is, the France of Catherine of Medici. Her efforts to guarantee the future of the kingdom of France and the successful reigns of her three king-sons would provoke her bringing into reality the Colloquy of Poissy. The Edict of Nantes was not yet declared by Henry IV. Théodore de Bèze was named by Calvin to lead the Reformed group at the Colloquy and to expose the tenets of the Reformation Church.

By the time of the declaration of the Edict of Nantes, Francis de Sales was exposing his Eucharist instruction through his life as priest missionary, co-founder of a contemplative religious community of women, and counter-reformation bishop. The Council of Trent had completed its session and set down the doctrines with which Roman churchmen, such as de Sales, would combat the Reform movement. This Salesian documentation is contained in the 26 volumes of the definitive edition of his works published by the Visitation community at Annecy. This source includes pamphlets, sermons, over 2,000 letters, conferences, several opuscules, but most particularly the two major spiritual writings of this author-bishop: namely, *The Introduction to the Devout Life* and *The Treatise on the Love of God*.

The two men met. Intriguing is the manner in which their encounters have come down to us in ensuing centuries. The Roman Catholic manner of hagiography of the 17th century presents us a very different narration from that of the Reformation historians. But this element briefly treated in a final chapter must await further development in a subsequent study. Here our subject is the Eucharist as presented by each of these 17th-century church leaders.

Here, suffice it to say, that each agreed basically on the notion of the Eucharist as sacrament even though their fundamental sacramental notions were different. Each accepted the real presence of Jesus Christ in the bread which was a sacramental sign. However, de Bèze's concept was that the presence of God was through the mysterious action of the Holy Spirit. Francis followed the Thomistic notion taught initially by Thomas Aquinas and implemented by the Council of Trent. This Tridentine doctrine would become the expression of the Church's Counter-Reformation teaching.

In our final chapter, we shall also examine three points of difference in the Reformation doctrine of de Bèze and the Counter-Reformation teachings of Francis de Sales. These issues involve the Eucharist as sacrament, the transubstantiation and finally the Eucharist as sacrifice. These doctrines distinguish typically the Eucharistic convictions of our two protagonists in their theological struggles.

It is in the analysis of the notion of the Eucharist as taught by Théodore de Bèze and by Francis de Sales that we hope to come to a greater knowledge and appreciation of the work of these two 17th-century leaders in their respective churches. In our contemporary period of ecumenical activity, such analyses and syntheses can have only positive effects in that which must be a sincere search for unity.

Théodore de Bèze (Peint sur bois) en 1577 Bibliothèque De Genève

CHAPTER I

Jean Calvin & Théodore de Bèze

Théodore de Bèze was a personally and dogmatically faithful friend and disciple of John Calvin. This is the reason that Calvin chose him as his successor at Geneva to lead a third generation of religious reformers. The absolute agreement of contemporary and successive generations attests vigorously and without rancor to this unique fidelity of de Bèze to his predecessor. Théodore de Bèze himself writes in his *De sacramentali corporis et sanguinis Christi cum sacris symbolis coniunctione...*: "Calvino optimo meo in Christo parente..."[1] attesting to the fact that he very fully realized the necessity of this fidelity to the transmission of the doctrine that had been passed to him from his beloved master. This fundamental point is shown in many writings on de Bèze. We shall choose only one of the latest here to illustrate this fact. A professor of history at the University of Geneva, Dr. Olivier Fatio wrote in 1985:

> Durant les neuf années de ce séjour lausannois, Bèze va révéler l'étendue de ses capacités; tour à tour polémiste et exégète, théologien systématique et versificateur, négociateur et diplomate, il s'imposera comme le premier des disciples de Calvin. Il est totalement acquis à la doctrine et à la personne de ce dernier, sans toutefois que sa soumission empêche le dialogue théologique. Malgre l'éloignement géographique, Bèze reste tourné vers Genève. Calvin pour sa part, s'attache rapidement et profondément à ce disciple.[2]

1. Bèze, Théodore de. *Opera.* (Genève, 1560) p. 88.

2. Fatio, O. *Théodore de Bèze ou les débuts de l'orthodoxie réformée. Hokhma*, 1985, pp. 2-3.

2

It is in this perspective then that a study of the Eucharist in the work of Théodore de Bèze begins by underlining the fact that Calvin's doctrine of the Eucharist was the essential teaching to which Théodore de Bèze remained faithful right up to the very end of his life when he dealt with the Eucharist in preaching and writing. The compendium of the doctrine of John Calvin is the *Institutions*. It is in this work where the Reformer initially sets down his teaching on the Eucharist. François Wendel recalls this compendium of Calvin's doctrine in the *Institutions* at the opening of his section on *The Theological Doctrine*.[3]

He quotes Imbart de la Tour:

> The whole of Calvinism is the *Institutes* - a work of capital importance, the work most valued by Calvin, who spent all his life revising and reshaping as well as enriching it. All his other works - commentaries, controversies, smaller dogmatic or moral treatises - are related to it like advanced redoubts meant to defend the heart of the place against the enemy.[4]

Calvin began then to write about the Eucharist beginning in 1536 in his first edition of the *Christian Institutions* and continued writing about it until the last edition in 1559. He treated this same question in the Articles of 1537[5] and in the *Confession of Faith* of 1537[6] as well as in his *Letter to Sadolet*

---

3.   Wendel, F. *Calvin: The Origins and Development of his Religious Thought.* (London: Collins, 1963) p. 111.

4.   Imbart de la Tour. *Calvin et l'Institution chrétienne.* (Paris, 1935) p. 55.

5.   The *Articles* begin in the following manner:

> Nous sommes Très honorés Seigneurs. Il est certain qu'une église ne peut être dite bien ordonnée et réglée sinon en laquelle la Sainte Cène de notre Seigneur est souventfois célébrée et fréquentée.... Le premier article précise cette pensée: "Il serait bien à desirer que la communication de la sainte Céne de Jésus-Christ fût tous les dimanches pour le moins en usage, quand l'eglise est assemblée en multitude, vu la grande consolation que les fidèles en reçoivent et le fruit qui en procède en toute manière. Quant à la foi de la Cène, il ajoute, c'est que vraiment nous sommes faits participants du corps et du sang de Jésus, de sa mort, de sa vie, de son Esprit et de tous ses biens. Dominice, M., *Calvin, homme d'Eglise.* Genève: Labor & Fides, 1971, 2d ed. pp. 1-13.

in 1537.[7] But it is especially in his *Petit Traité sur la Sainte Cène* in 1541 that he proposed a solution to the question of the Eucharist which divided the Protestant camp since 1529. It is this document that presents in brief compass the essential features of Calvin's eucharistic doctrine in relation to the eucharistic doctrine of others. Théodore de Bèze used this writing as a basis for his own faithful transmission of that doctrine passed to him from Calvin. His own orthodox manner of re-presenting the thought of his master to a succeeding generation is true not only in the teaching on the Eucharist but also in other areas of the Reformer's essential doctrines.

Professor at La Faculté de Théologie Protestante de Montpellier, Jean Cadier, has written that this *Petit Traité* is "un chef d'oeuvre de clarté et

---

6.   We cite Chapter XVI here:

> La Cène de notre Seigneur est un signe par lequel sous le pain et le vin il nous représente la vraie communication spirituelle que nous avons en son corps et son sang. Et reconnaissons que, selon son ordonnance, elle doit être distribuée en la compagnie des fidèles, afin que tous ceux qui veulent avoir Jésus pour leur vie en soient participants. Or, d'autant que la messe du pape a été une ordonnance maudite et diabolique pour renverser le mystère de cette sainte Cène, nous déclarons qu'elle nous est en exécration, comme une idolâtrie condamnée de Dieu, tant en ce qu'elle est estimée un sacrifice pour la rédemption des âmes que pour ce que le pain est en icelle de tenu et adoré comme Dieu; outre les autres blasphèmes et superstitions exécrables qui y sont contenues, et l'abus de la Parole de Dieu, qui y est prise en vain sans aucun fruit ni édification. Dominice, M., *Calvin, Homme d'Eglise*, pp. 22-23.

7.   Calvin refutes here the accusation that the Cardinal made of the Reformers saying:

> d'enclore le seigneur du ciel de la terre et enserrer sa puissance spirituelle, qui est libre et infinie, dans les anglets d'un corps humain, qui est environné de ses fins et à certaines proportions...Et toi, tu n'a point honte de nous reprocher d'avoir enclos (la divine puissance de Christ) dans les proportions d'un corps naturel. Pourquoi cela? Parce que nous n'avons pas voulu, comme vous, assujettir son corps à des choses visibles et terriennes. Schmidt, A.-M. *Epître à Sadolet, Trois Traités.* Paris: Je Sers, 1934, p. 63.

4

de spiritualité."[8] It is very well organized and written. Calvin's extraordinary intelligence and humanistic formation are easily discernible in its content as well as in its form. For these reasons, then, we shall analyze this radical eucharistic definition of Calvin in order to understand clearly the teaching that Théodore de Bèze made his own.

The first two paragraphs of the *Traité*[9] present us the double motive which had incited Calvin to write, as well as the order he intended to follow.[10] First "beaucoup de consciences informes" have "nulle certitude de ce mystère." That, for him, is "une chose fort périlleuse," because the understanding of this mystery is "tant requise à notre salut." Furthermore, "aucuns bons personnages" ask him his opinion regarding this question.

The questions treated involve five points:

A.   A quelle fin et pour quelle raison le Seigneur nous a institué ce sainct Sacrament?

B.   Quel fruict et utilité nous en recevons?

C.   Quel en est l'usage légitime?

D.   De quelz erreurs et superstition il a esté contaminé?

E.   Quelle a esté la source de la contention?

A.   *INSTITUTION OF THE EUCHARIST*

We shall deal in two parts with the paragraphs by which Calvin exposes the end and the reason for the existence of the sacrament:[11] *First,* that Jesus Christ is the only spiritual nourishment and *secondly,* that we participate in the body and the blood of Christ.

1.   Jesus Christ is our only spiritual nourishment:

a.   The spiritual life and spiritual nourishment:

8.   Cadier, J. *La doctrine calviniste de la sainte Cène.* (Montpellier, 1951) p. 8.

9.   Schmidt, A.-M. *Trois Traités*, p. 103.

10.   *Ibid.*

11.   *Ibid.*, pp. 106-109.

After baptism, the Christian life begins. It is by baptism that God receives us into his Church "comme ses propres enfants." Baptism can be considered as the origin of the new life, but it is only the exterior sign of regeneration. The beginning of the spiritual life "c'est quand, en nous adoptant pour ses enfants, il nous a régénérés par la semence d'immortalité qui est sa parole, imprimée en nos coeurs par son Esprit."

Subsequent upon the regeneration is the spiritual life. As in the case of physical life, it is after birth that the child needs nourishment. The spiritual life is comparable. As corporal man needs bodily nutrition, so also the spiritual man needs spiritual nutrition. "Tout ainsi, says Calvin, que la vie en laquelle il nous a régénérés est spirituelle: aussi faut-il que la viande, pour nous conserver et confirmer en icelle, soit spirituelle." Effectively, corporal nourishment is not peculiar to the family of God because it is "commune à tous, et que les mauvais en ont leur part comme les bons."

      b.   Jesus Christ, our spiritual bread:

So it is then, that, for our spiritual life, it does not concern physical nourishment, but the "pature meilleure et plus précieuse." Now this spiritual food is "la même parole par laquelle le Seigneur nous a régénérés" and in which "Jesus Christ nous est donné." It is difficult to outline the relation between God-word-Jesus Christ-us. The thought of Calvin seems to be that God has ordered the word as instrument, by which, on the one hand, He regenerates us. On the other hand, He gives us the fullness of life which is in Jesus Christ; although we receive Jesus Christ in His word, He is always the only source of our nutrition. "Nos âmes n'ont nulle autre pâture" than He. To nourish us, God "ne nous en donne point d'autre."[12]

      2.   We share in the body and blood of Christ.

Having said that Jesus Christ is our only nourishment, Calvin progresses to our sharing in this nourishment. As he said above, Jesus Christ is given to us by the word of God. However "nous sommes si imbéciles que nous ne le pouvons pas recevoir en vraie fiance de coeur," "par simple doctrine et prédiction." Furthermore, "c'est un mystère tant haut et incompréhensible de dire que nous ayons communication au corps et au sang

---

12.   *Ibid.*, p. 105.

de Jesus Christ." That is why God has willed to accommodate us in our infirmity and "ajouter avec sa parole un signe visible," that is, "pain et eau." It is by this means, according to our capacity, that God "nous mène à la communication de Jesus Christ."

Finishing these paragraphs, Calvin points out three reasons for Christ's instituting the Eucharist. That is, first, in order to "sceller en nos consciences les promesses" of the Gospel and to give us the certainty that our true spiritual food resides in the body and blood of Christ; next, to accustom us to recognizing, praising and glorifying his goodness; finally, in order to exhort us to every holiness and innocence especially to union and fraternal charity.[13]

B.   *FRUIT AND UTILITY OF THE EUCHARIST*

For a greater clarity, we shall divide this section into three parts:
1.   Through the Eucharist we possess Jesus Christ and all his riches.
2.   The Eucharist incites us to the praise of God.
3.   The Eucharist exhorts us to live in a holy manner.

1.   Through the Eucharist we possess Jesus Christ and all his riches:

Calvin begins by considering our indigence and misery in order to contrast it with our possession of the fullness of grace in Christ. In this exposition he clarifies two things:

First, the substance and the efficacy of the Eucharist, and *secondly*, the relation between the bread and wine and then between the bread and the wine and the body and the blood.

a.   In ourselves we are incapable:

Another aspect of the theology to which de Bèze will be faithful is Calvin's view of man. It is this anthropological point of departure which the Reformers, in general, practice. That is, theirs is a view of man which emphasizes the radicality of sin as opposed to the Roman Catholic position on sin as a wounding.[14] Calvin thinks that man cannot merit his own

---

13.   *Ibid.*, pp. 105-106.

14.   Marceau, W. *L'optimisme dans les oeuvres de saint François de Sales.* (Paris, 1973) pp. 226-255.

salvation. No man can find "un seul grain de justice en soi," nor "une seule goutte des choses qui nous doivent aider à salut," but "nous sommes tous pleins de péché et iniquité." It is our conscience which accuses and condemns us. "Il n'y a nul qui puisse échapper de la mort éternelle." This must lead us to a kind of hell: "nous vexer et tourmenter." Hence it is that if we look at ourselves in a frank and truthful manner, we discover that "nous sommes plus que misérables." The awareness of such misery has to lead us to a real sadness.[15]

   b.   The Eucharist makes up for our incapacity:

To make up for our misery, God gives us the Eucharist. For Calvin the Eucharist is like a mirror by which we contemplate the crucified and risen Christ. He died "pour abolir nos fautes et offenses, et ressucité pour nous délivrer de corruption et de mort." It is the Eucharist which leads us to the certainty that God justifies us, vivifies and fills us with joy in spite of our iniquity. This iniquity is the cause of our death and misfortune. In other words, in face of our own misery, "elle nous rend témoinage qu'étant faits participants de la mort et passion de Jesus Christ, nous avons tout ce qui nous est utile et salutaire." Present in the Eucharist are "tous les trésors de ses grâces spirituelles."

Calvin applies the word "miroir" figuratively to the Eucharist as "lunettes" to the word of God.[16] The Eucharist and the word of God are both God's instruments by which we receive his grace. But for Calvin, it is in the Eucharist that "nous en avons plus ample certitude et pleine jouissance."

   c.   Substance and efficacy of the Eucharist:

Next the Reformer distinguishes the substance of the Eucharist from its efficacy without separating one from the other. He affirms that we cannot possess all the spiritual graces of Christ unless we do the same thing. "Il faut qu'en premier lieu il nous soit donné en la Cène." This is also in order that all his good and his riches be ours. For Calvin, the substance[17] of the

---

15.   For example, *Institutions*, I, VI, I. Also cf. Stauffer, R., *Dieu,, la création et la Providence dans la prédication de Calvin.* (Berne, 1978) p. 53.

16.   Schmidt, A.-M., pp. 107-108.

17.   For the use of "substance" by Calvin, cf., Cadier, J. *Op. cit.*, pp. 24-25.

8

Eucharist (the sacrament) is the Lord Jesus, and the efficacy of the Eucharist (the sacrament) consists in our graces and blessings. Since the efficacity of the Eucharist proceeds from the work of Christ: "sa mort et passion," "l'effusion de son sang," "son obéissance," that is "tout ce qu'il a fait pour nous," "il faut donc que la substance soit conjointe avec (l'efficace)."

Having concluded that "deux choses nous sont présentées en la Cène: à savoir Jesus Christ, comme source et matière de tout bien; puis après, le fruit et efficace de la mort et passion."[18] Calvin takes up the question that became so very important, namely "comment doivent être comprises les paroles d'institution?"

> d.   Relationship between the bread and wine and the body and blood:

When Jesus Christ "en nous commandant de manger son corps et boire son sang," adds that "son corps a été livré pour nous et son sang épandu pour la rémission de nos échecs," and he points out "que nous ne devons pas simplement communiquer à son corps et a son sang sans autre considération mais recevoir le fruit," and "que nous ne pouvons parvenir à la jouissance d'un tel fruit, qu'en participant à son corps et à son sang." Now in these words of institution, the bread is called the body of Christ and the wine his blood. How should this be understood?

For the Reformer, Jesus Christ is truly or really given in the Eucharist. "De nier la vraie communication de Jesus Christ nous être présentée en la Cène, c'est rendre ce saint Sacrement frivole et inutile, qui est un blasphème exécrable et indigne d'être écouté." It is Calvin's intention to affirm the real presence of Christ in the Eucharist. For him, we participate not only in the spirit of Christ, but also in his humanity which includes the body and the blood. As "son Esprit est notre vie," "sa chair est vraiment viande, son sang vraiment breuvage." It is in the Eucharist that our souls are satiated with his body and blood. The bread that we take and eat is his body. The wine that we drink is his blood.

---

18.   Schmidt, A.-M., pp. 108-109.

But to avoid too literal an interpretation, Calvin quickly adds that "le pain et le vin sont signes visibles, lesquels nous représent le corps et le sang." It is precisely at this point that Calvin finds the mystery of the Eucharist. The communion with Christ is, in effect, such an incomprehensible thing that God has shown it to us visibly. In order to justify his theory, the Reformer presents a biblical example "bien propre en chose semblable": the descent of the Holy Spirit at the baptism of Christ. While seeing a dove descend, John the Baptist knows that this is "un signe certain de la présence du Saint Esprit" and is not afraid to say: "qu'il l'à vu, pour ce qu'il s'est représenté à lui selon sa capacité."

It is in this same way that Christ, because of our incapacity, is represented to us by the bread and the wine. However, it is not "une figure nue mais conjointe avec sa vérité et substance." Between the substance and the representation, there is not any separation, but there is a distinction. "Les Sacrements du Seigneur ne se doivent et ne peuvent nullement être séparés de leur vérité et substance." To distinguish them is absolutely necessary in order not to confuse them. The bread and the wine are given to us in order to represent the body and blood of Christ. We are commanded to consume them. Calvin indicates the relationship between the sign and the substance by saying: "La substance intérieure du Sacrement est conjointe avec les signes visibles: et comme le pain nous est distribué en la main, aussi le corps du Christ nous est communiqué, afin que nous soyons faits participants."

Finally, Calvin defines this first use of the Eucharist in affirming that "Jesus Christ nous y (dans la Cène) est offert, afin que nous le possédions, et en lui toute plénitude des grâces que nous pouvons désirer."[19]

2.   The Eucharist encourages giving praise:

We receive daily the goods of the Lord Jesus. However, we are too negligent to consider the goodness of God, "sinon qu'il réveille notre paresse." For this reason God has given us an "aiguillon" to make us more sensitive: "c'est de nous repaître de sa propre substance." This is why Jesus Christ has commanded us to celebrate the Eucharist until the moment that

---

19.   *Ibid.*, pp. 109-113.

he comes to us again. Calvin considers this the second use of the Sacrament. The Eucharist rids us of our ingratitude, it recalls to us "le bien que nous a fait le Seigneur Jesus" and invites us "à lui rendre action des grâces," publicly confessing how we are joined to Him.[20]

3.   The Eucharist exhorts us to live well in fraternal charity:
The Reformer advances still further in the third use of the Eucharist. This step will be into the area of our sanctification. In so far as we are members of Jesus Christ, "c'est bien raison premièrement que nous soyons faits conformes à sa pureté et innocence," and especially "que nous ayons ensemble telle charité et concorde comme doivent avoir les membres d'un même corps." Here Calvin adds the necessity of the interior aid of the Holy Spirit. This doctrine is going to be very important. "Il ne faut pas estimer que notre Seigneur nous avertisse. . . nos coeurs par le signe extérieur seulement," because "il besogne en nous intérieurement par son Saint Esprit, a fin de rendre efficace son ordonnance. . . ." It is because "la vertu du Saint Esprit est conjointe aux Sacrements" that we should believe that the Eucharist is "un bon moyen et aide" for our holiness of life and especially our fraternal charity.[21]

C.   THE LEGITIMATE USE OF THE EUCHARIST

We have already seen that Calvin teaches that God instituted the Eucharist in order to give us spiritual nourishment. Jesus Christ is that nourishment as the substance of the Sacrament. By reception of Jesus Christ in this Sacrament, we possess all his riches and we are called to praise Him and to live in a holy way in fraternal charity. Having established, therefore, the nature of this Sacrament, Calvin asks some practical questions: for example, how should one receive the Eucharist? For him, to participate in the Eucharist "avec mépris ou nonchalence," is to contaminate it. This is "un sacrilège intolérable." One must not take the body and blood of the Lord without being well prepared.

---

20.   *Ibid.*, p. 113.

21.   *Ibid.*, p. 114.

1.   How should we participate in the Eucharist?

a.   We must prepare interiorly in our heart:

To achieve this we must know "si nous avons vraie repentance en nous-mêmes et vraie foi en notre Seigneur Jesus Christ." These two elements are "tellement conjointes que l'une ne peut consister sans l'autre."

This is the first preparation principle. This sentiment of a true repentance based on faith ought to engender the three following results: "un déplaisir de toute notre vie," "une inquiétude et crainte," "un désir et amour de justice." Once again Calvin speaks here of our miserable condition without God. However, he adds that in tasting the goodness of God, we desire "renoncer à toute notre vie passée pour être faits en lui de nouvelles créatures." The "vrai sentiment de nostre misère" leads our hearts not only to be confident in Jesus in order to properly receive the Eucharist, but also to have a hunger and thirst for him. The third result is a positive one: to aspire to God's justice "laquelle se trouve en l'abnégation de nous-mêmes et dans l'obéissance à sa volonté." In order to participate in Christ's body, in which "il n'y a que chasteté, bénignité, sobriété, vérité, humilité et toutes les vertus semblables," we must avoid all vices, iniquities and debaucheries. This is because the light and darkness cannot be mixed in Christ.[22]

b.   Friendship among the members of Christ:

It is especially in the Eucharist that we must show our charity. It is for this reason that this sacrament is called the "bond of charity." Calvin gives us a lovely image of the bread and our friendship: "comme le pain qui est la sanctifié pour l'usage commun de tous nous, est fait de plusieurs grains tellement mêlés ensemble qu'on ne sauroit discerner l'un de l'autre, ainsi devons-nous être unis entre nous d'une amitié indissoluble." This is probably of Lutheran origin.[23] Jesus Christ must not be dismembered because of our dissensions and our discord. That is why when we receive the Eucharist, we must leave behind us any hatred or bad feeling towards our fellow Christians, for this "amitié" constitutes the unity of the Church.[24]

---

22.   *Ibid.*, pp. 114-117.

23.   Wendel, F., *op. cit.*, p. 252.

24.   Schmidt, A.-M., p. 118.

c. External confession:

Finally, Calvin adds "une autre affection" which is the third element in preparation for the Eucharist. That is to confess orally our relation with Christ, not only to glorify him but also in order to "édifier les autres et les instruire par notre exemple de ce qu'ils ont à faire."[25]

2. Our weakness does not remove the Eucharist from us.

a. The perilous perfection:

Having established the conditions necessary for receiving the Eucharist, Calvin then indicates that some type of perfection must exist in the communicant. This is because he sees in certain persons a perilous method of teaching to "requérir une parfaite fiance de coeur et parfaite pénitence de coeur et parfaite pénitence, et exclure de la Cène tous ceux qui ne l'ont point." No one could participate in the Eucharist if this policy were followed. Therefore, Calvin asks: "Qui sera celui qui se puisse vanter de n'être entaché de quelque défiance?, de n'être sujet à quelque vice ou infirmité?" Actually, Calvin is not a perfectionist. For him the weakness of the children of God does not stop them from presenting themselves at the table of the Lord, but on the contrary, they find there a unique remedy for their weakness.[26]

b. No hypocrisy:

We know that Calvin has affirmed that Christ and iniquity cannot be together. But he states expressly: "qu'il n'y ait point d'hypocrisie." In effect, our "maladie" is so "enracinée en notre nature que jamais nous n'en sommes pleinement guéris," before being delivered "de cette prison de notre corps." And then, the true repentance is accomplished "non pas pour un jour ou pour une semaine," but for our whole life, when we do battle constantly "contre le mal qui est en nous."[27]

c. In order to receive without hypocrisy:

We are fit to partake in the Eucharist, notwithstanding the remains of sin in our flesh, when we feel within ourselves a "firm displeasure and hatred

25. *Ibid.*

26. *Ibid.*

27. *Ibid.*, p. 119.

of all vice, proceeding from the fear of God and a desire to live well in order to please our Lord." If not, the preparations he has underlined above would lose their validity. True faith and true repentance satisfy this condition. If, then, we have true faith the true repentance, we are capable of participating in the Holy Supper. A double witness is required: the interior witness by faith and the exterior by repentance.[28]

       3.   Frequency of celebration and of reception of the Eucharist:

           a.   The Eucharist ought to be celebrated often:

Calvin exhorts his followers to celebrate the Eucharist "souvent." The Reformer reasons that the end of the Sacrament encourages its frequent use; the end being that it "peut et doit nous servir à nous confirmer en Foi et avancer en pureté de vie." Furthermore, he observes that many do not receive at the altar. So he affirms that "cette coutume doit être, en toutes Eglises bien ordonnées, de célébrer souvent la Cène, tant que la capacité du peuple le peut porter," and that "chacun particulier se doit préparer à la recevoir" each time that he participates in the Eucharist.

           b.   Three types of Christians who do not often receive:

Calvin divides into three categories those who abstain:

           1) Those who consider themselves unworthy
           2) Those who do not want to receive with those whom they conside unworthy
           3) Those who think that once having received Jesus Christ, it is superfluous to receive again.

The Reformer comments on these categories in the following manner:

       (1)   For the first group, Calvin does not deny "qu'il soit loisible de différer à cause d'une cause légitime qui empêche." But in abstaining from the Eucharist over a long period, they sever themselves from the communion of the church. He advised them to be strong and "combattre contre tous les empêchements."

       (2)   Calvin recognizes the legitimacy of the argument of the second group. But he replies that "ce n'est pas le moyen de nous retirer de la compagnie des méchants, en quittant la communion de l'Eglise." It is not the

---

28.   *Ibid.*, pp. 119-120.

14

responsibility of an individual to "juger et discerner pour admettre ou déchasser qui bon lui semble." This is rather an ecclesiastical responsibility.

(3)   As for the third group, Calvin refutes them in saying that "le pain spirituel ne nous est pas donné afin que nous en soûlions du premier coup," but rather "afin qu'en ayant quelque goût de sa douceur, nous appétions davantage et en usions quand il nous est offert." The Eucharist is, then, our "nourriture continuelle.[29]

D.   *ERRORS AND SUPERSTITIONS REGARDING THE EUCHARIST*

Théodore de Bèze was of the same mind as was Calvin regarding the eucharistic practices of the Roman Church. After having presented the institution of the Cène, its fruits and its legitimate use, the Reformer criticizes in this *Treatise* those practices which he considers erroneous. He deals first with the Roman Mass which he attacks rather violently. Subsequently he treats certain Protestant practices of Luther and other Reformers.

1.   The institution of the Lord and the invention of men:

a.   The goal of the institution of the Eucharist is to attest:

"qu'en communiquant à son corps, nous avons part au Sacrifice qu'il a offert en la croix à Dieu." What did certain men invent? They conceived a Sacrifice "par lequel nous acquérons la rémission de nos péchés devant Dieu." To distinguish the institution from the invention, Calvin presents two points as criteria: "la mort du Seigneur Jésus comme un Sacrifice unique" and Jesus Christ as the one offering. Therefore, the invention of men does not respond to the criteria established. Thus it must be condemned as diabolical.

b.   The ceremony of the ancient Church:

The error appeared from the beginning, but "n'a pas été du premier coup tant extrême." The ancient Fathers called the Eucharist a sacrifice, because "la mort de Jesus Christ y est représentée." For Calvin they are right in so far as the Eucharist is "la mémoire de ce sacrifice unique." The Reformer considers that the custom and the ceremony of the ancient Church

---

29.   *Ibid.*, pp. 121-123.

are too veterotestamentary; that is, those of Judaism. In effect, the ceremonies of the Old Testament have been figures before Jesus Christ accomplished them. But since the sacrifice has become perfect on the cross, it is superfluous to present it again as in the "temps des figures." Hence, it is no longer a question of offering or of immolating, but of taking and eating "ce qui a été offert et immolé."[30]

c.   The error of the sacrifice of the Mass:

Calvin thinks that the ancient Church has not had "une impiété telle qu'elle est depuis survenue." Increasingly there has been transferred to the Mass all that which was proper to the death of Christ: to render to God satisfaction for our debts and to become reconciled with Him. Furthermore, the priests have replaced the office of Jesus Christ as the one offering the sacrifice and as intercessor. "Les ennemis de vérité" allege that "la Messe n'est pas un sacrifice nouveau, mais seulement une application du sacrifice unique." But this is only pure subtlety. Where is the error of the sacrifice of the Mass? It is precisely at that point where one ignores that the sacrifice of Christ must never again be performed because the original was unique and consequently one must not again offer the same oblation; that is exactly where one accords the merit of the death of Christ to the Mass. As for the manner of applying to ourselves the merit of his death, that is done by the message of the Gospel which is preached to us in sermons and sealed by sacraments.[31]

d.   There is no communion in the Mass:

Thus it is that Calvin declares that "toutes Messes, auxquelles il n'y a point de communion telle que le Siegneur l'a instituée, ne sont qu'abomination." And he deplores the unfortunate custom of the Roman Church "que le peuple se contente d'assister là pour participer au mérite de ce qui s'y fait à cause que le prêtre se vante d'offrir son hostie pour tous, et spécialement pour les assistants."[32]

---

30.   *Ibid.*, pp. 123-125.

31.   *Ibid.*, pp. 125-126.

32.   *Ibid.*, p. 127.

2.   Transubstantiation:

a.   The error of Transubstantiation:

The second error concerning the Eucharist is the invention of the doctrine of "transubstantiation" which means that the bread changes its substance into the body of Christ, and the wine into His blood. The Reformer looks for the refutation of "ce mensonge" in the words of Jesus Christ when he instituted the Sacrament and in a comparison that uses the text of St. Paul (I Cor.: X, 17). In this particular treatment of the subject, he neglects to use the witness of the ancient Church. In doing all this, he simply wants to show that "la nature du Sacrement requiert que le pain matériel demeure du pain pour signe visible du corps"; in other words, that there be a similitude between the corporal element and the spiritual element. For him, it is the same as in the case of Baptism.[33]

b.   The words of Christ at the institution of the Sacrament:

Calvin always returns to Jesus' words of institution as did Luther, but Calvin's interpretation is quite different from that of Luther. Our Reformer shows that the bread remains truly bread in interpreting Jesus' words in the following manner: "Tout ainsi que l'homme est sustenté et entretenu selon le corps en mangeant du pain, ainsi ma chair est la nourriture spirituelle dont les âmes sont vivifiées."[34]

c.   Paul's comparison:

Furthermore, the word of God denies transubstantiation. Paul tells us, in I Cor., X, 17, that "comme plusieurs grains de blé sont mêlés ensemble pour faire un pain, ainsi faut-il que nous soyons unis ensemble, puisque nous participons tous d'un pain." "La blancheur sans substance" contradicts this concept.

This is the reason that "cette transubstantiation est une invention forgée par le Diable."[35]

---

33.   *Ibid.*

34.   *Ibid.*, p. 128.

35.   *Ibid.*

3.   The local presence:

a.   The imagination of the local presence:

This imaginative doctrine of transubstantiation even goes to the point of conceiving of local presence: Jesus Christ is contained under the signs. In order to support this theory, one must believe one of two things: either "que le corps du Christ est sans mesure," or "qu'il peut être en divers lieux." The first is the opinion of Luther that is called the doctrine of ubiquity. Calvin does not want to accept this local presence because it leads to the notion that the body of Christ "ne diffère en rien d'un Phantasme." He flatly states that to wish to establish local presence, "c'est non seulement une rêverie, mais une erreur damnable."[36]

b.   The truth of Christ's humanity and the glory of his Ascension:

It is clear here that Calvin approaches closely to the doctrine of Zwingli. He recommends that we consider two things concerning Christ's humanity: "c'est que nous ne lui (Christ) ôtons pas le vérité de sa nature, et que nous ne dérogeons rien à sa condition glorieuse." Scripture shows us that Jesus Christ has human nature and that He is in glory after His Ascension. For Calvin, it is "notre entendement," or our reason that has imagined, "sans regarder au ciel," this "rêverie diabolique."[37]

c.   Other superstitions:

This perverse opinion (local presence) has engendered many other superstitions.

First, this has brought about the carnal adoration of Christ vis-à-vis the bread. But "se prosterner devant le pain de la Cène et là adorer Jesus Christ. . . c'est en faire un idole, au lieu d'un sacrement." Furthermore, this involves "porter en pompe le Sacrement par les rues," and to "le garder en une armoire." All this must be rejected because it is contrary to the word of God and to the institution of the Eucharist.[38]

---

36.   *Ibid.*, pp. 128-129.

37.   *Ibid.*, pp. 129-130.

38.   *Ibid.*, pp. 130-131.

4.   Communion under one species:

    a.   As we know, the Roman Church for many centuries distributed communion to the faithful only in the form of bread:

In recalling that, Calvin determined that the Eucharist was "pauvrement dissipée et comme déchirée en pièces." People had to be content with receiving half the Sacrament without receiving "le Sacrement du sang." The Reformer declares without hesitating that "le Pape a tyrannisé l'Eglise. C'est une trop grand cruauté, de le ravir à ceux auxquels il appartient." Our Lord has expressly commanded: "Buvez tous!" (Mt, XXVI, 27). But the Pope dares to say: "N'en buvez pas tous!"[39]

    b.   Excuses of the papists:
       1)   "Si le calice était communément donné à tous," there would be the danger of spilling it.

But Calvin thinks that this is to accuse God of having confounded "l'ordre qu'il devait observer et mis son peuple en danger sans propos."

       2)   The Pope defines that "sous une espèce tout est compris, d'autant que le corps ne peut être divisé du sang." But why then had the Lord distinguished the one from the other?
       3)   "Certain de ses suppôts" say that "Jesus Christ, en instituant le Sacrement, ne parlait qu'à ses Apôtres, qu'il avait érigés en ordre sacerdotal." Calvin replies to them, in the words of St. Paul: that Paul "a baillé à tout le peuple Chrétien ce qu'il avait reçu du Seigneur" that all should eat this bread and drink this cup.

Then Calvin concludes that "c'est une perversité intolérable de diviser ainsi et déchirer le sacrement, séparant les parties que Dieu a conjointes."[40]

5.   The Mass is a monkey-like imitation and subterfuge:

    a.   The Mass is a monkey-like imitation:

Why an imitation: Calvin replies: "Pour ce qu'on veut là contre-faire la Cène du Seigneur, sans raison, comme un singe, inconsidérément et sans discrétion, ensuite (imite) ce qu'il voit faire." But the Lord recommends us to "celébrer ce mystère avec vraie intelligence." The substance lies, therefore, in the doctrine and not in the ceremony. According to Holy

---

39.   *Ibid.*, p. 131.

40.   *Ibid.*, pp. 131-132.

Scripture and according to the ancient Fathers, particularly St. Augustine, it is clear that "les Sacrements prennent leur vertu de la parole, quand elle est prêchée intelligiblement." The Sacraments without the word "ne sont pas dignes qu'on les nomme Sacrement." This is the case with the Mass. As for its consecration, this is a sort of witchcraft, because as do witches "en murmurant et faisant beaucoup de signes," these "Mass-sayers" want "contraindre Jesus Christ de descendre entre leurs mains." Thus the Mass is "une profanation évident de la Cène du Christ" and is deprived of its "propre et principale substance."[41]

      b.   The Mass is a subterfuge:

Calvin calls the Mass a subterfuge: "les fatras et mines qu'on fait conviennent plutôt à une farce qu'à un tel mystère" such as the Eucharist. The "Mass-sayers," in order to defend their ceremonies, allege that they follow the example of the Old Testament whose sacrifices were performed with different trappings and ceremonies. This is the reason that Calvin clarifies the difference between the sacrifices of the Old Testament and that of the Mass. Those of the people of Israel were founded on the commandement of the Lord, but that of the Mass has absolutely "nul fondement que les hommes." Furthermore, "depuis que Jesus Christ a été manifesté en chair," everything has been fulfilled and "les figures ont été diminuées," because they were given for a time. We must "délaisser les ombres." If not, we refabricate "le voile du temple que Jesus Christ a rompu par sa mort, et obscurcir la clarté de son Evangile." Hence, the Mass is "une forme de Juiverie qui est pleinement contraire à la Chrétienté." Therefore, it is only a farce because the abolished ceremonies are being used again.[42]

      6.   Résumé: five points against the Mass:

The Reformer sums up then in five points all that he has just developed regarding the errors and the superstitions dealing with the Eucharist. He does this to render more certain "ceux à qui Dieu a donné intelligence de sa vérité."

---

41.   *Ibid.*, pp. 133-134.

42   *Ibid.*, pp. 134-135.

20

a. They...must not doubt that it is an abominable sacrilege to think that the Mass as a sacrifice remits our sins by the intermediary of the priest. On the contrary, they must hold to the unique sacrifice in the death and the passion of the Lord Jesus, who after having entered "au Sanctuaire céleste" intercedes for us "avec la vertu de de son sacrifice." Then they must concede that "le fruit de cette mort nous est communiqué," not by the merit of our works, but by the promises which are given us in the Supper, provided we receive them in faith.[43]

b. "Ils...ne doivent nullement accorder que le pain soit transsubstantié au corps de Jesus Christ ni le vin en son sang," but must maintain that "les signes visibles retiennent leur vraie substance pour nous représenter la vérité spirituelle."[44]

c. Even though, in the Eucharist, believers truly receive the body and the blood of Christ, nevertheless, they must not search for him as if he were attached locally to the visible sign, but raise "leurs entendements et leurs coeurs en haut, tant pour recevoir Jesus Christ que pour l'adorer." They must condemn all superstitious practices which flow from this real presence: "de porter le Sacrement en pompe et procession, et de lui construire des tabernacles pour le faire adorer."[45]

d. They must maintain that "priver le peuple d'une des parties du Sacrement, à savior du calice, c'est violer et

---

43. *Ibid.*, p. 135.

44. *Ibid.*, p. 136.

45. *Ibid.*

corrompre l'ordonnance du Seigneur," and that it is necessary "de distribuer entièrement l'un et l'autre."[46]

e. They must consider that "c'est une superfluité, non seulement inutile, mais aussi dangereuse et mal convenable à la Chrétienté d'user de tant ce cérémonies prises des Juifs," and that it is a still greater perversity "de célébrer la Cène par mines" without recalling the doctrine, as if it were a sort of magic art.[47]

E. *THE PROTESTANT CONTROVERSY*

Calvin terminates the *Treatise* with the subject of the Protestant controversy on the Eucharist. This controversy so bitterly waged was a great disappointment to Calvin who actually belongs to the second generation of the Reform. He only desires that it could be abolished from memory. However, de Bèze, who will be of the third generation, seeks not to abolish the struggle from his correligionists' memory, but desires that he and they be faithful to the evolution that the two preceding generations have left them. Calvin recounts a history of the conflict in order to give his followers an idea of what has led him to write the *Treatise*.

It might be well here, in trying to appreciate the inheritance of Théodore de Bèze to terminate this section with the historical sketch that Calvin etches at the end of *Le Petit Traité sur la sainte Cène*.

1.   Luther and his fault:

For Calvin, the error of Luther lay in his explanation of the real presence. In effect, Luther left the corporal presence "elle que le monde la concevait pour lors" in affirming the consubstantiation. In order to explain his notion, "il ajoutait des similitudes, lesquelles étaient un peu dures et rudes." It is precisely against this concept of the carnal presence that had been "enseignée et tenue plus de six cent ans" that Zwingli and Oecolampade react. Was it not, as Calvin has already shown in the preceding paragraphs,

---

46.   *Ibid.*, pp. 136-137.

47.   *Ibid.*, p. 138.

that "Jesus Christ y était adoré comme enclos sous le pain?" But Calvin, it seems to me, hesitates to criticize Luther, for he says that the Reformer of Wittenberg "le faisait comme par contrainte, pour ce qu'il ne pouvait autrement expliquer son intention."[48]

2.   Zwingli, Oecolampade and their error:

Zwingli and Oecolampade, in order to get rid of the concept of the carnal presence "enracinée si longtemps au coeur des hommes," applied "tout leur entendement à l'encontre." But in emphasizing the importance of the Ascension of Jesus, "ils oubliaient de montrer quelle présence de Jesus Christ on doit croire en la Cène et quelle communication de son corps et de son sang on y reçoit." That is why Luther "pensait qu'ils ne voulussent laisser autre chose que les signes nus, sans leur substance spirituelle."

Thus the controversy began and endured "trop amèrement" for about fifteen years without any concession on the part of either side."[49]

3.   Failure of the Colloquy of Marburg:

At the conference, Luther's responsibility was triple: "admonester qu'il n'entendait pas établir une telle présence locale que les papistes la songent"; "protester qu'il ne voulait pas faire adorer le Sacrement au lieu de Dieu"; "s'abstenir de ses similitudes tant rudes et difficiles à concevoir." But once the debate was engaged "il a excédé mesure." Rather than expressing himself calmly, "il a usé de formes hyperboliques de parler" in blaming and accusing others.

Others offended him as well. They were "tellement acharnés à crier l'opinion superstitieuse et fantastique" of the papists' treatment of the local presence that they "se sont plus efforcés de ruiner le mal que d'édifier le bien." In this way they omitted adding that the bread and the wine "sont tellement signes que la vérité est conjointe avec" and to affirm "qu'ils ne prétendaient nullement d'obscurer vraie communion que nous donne le Seigneur en son corps et son sang par ce Sacrement."[50]

---

48.   *Ibid.*

49.   *Ibid.*, pp. 138-139.

50.   *Ibid.*, pp. 139-140.

Having evoked the difficulties that this problem had caused in the past, Calvin recommended agreement on this point to his followers. Just what effect did his recommendation have on his successor? I believe it had a telling effect. This I hope to demonstrate clearly in this study's final chapter.

Calvin's general conclusion to the *De Coena Domini* is a confession of faith: "Nous confessons donc tous d'une bouche, qu'en recevant en Foi le Sacrement, selon l'ordonnance du Seigneur, nous sommes vraiment faits participants de la proper substance du corps et du sang de Jesus Christ." We must "élever les coeurs en haut au ciel, ne pensant pas que le Seigneur Jésus soit abaissé jusque-là d'être enclos sous quelques éléments corruptibles. . . il nous fait penser que cela se fait par la vertu secrète et miraculeuse de Dieu, et que l'esprit de Dieu est le lien de cette participation, pour laquelle cause elle est appellée spirituelle."[51]

F.   *THÉODORE DE BÈZE AND THOMAS AQUINAS*

To this point, we have tried to accentuate the fact that Théodore de Bèze was a very faithful son of Calvin. This is the reason for having presented Calvin's doctrine of the Eucharist to which de Bèze was uniquely faithful as a relatively young theologian and leader of the Reformed movement. In our Chapter III we shall present several works of de Bèze which will manifest that he remained a remarkably faithful transmitter of Calvin's eucharistic teachings.

Dublanchy presents the systematic writings of de Bèze in the *Dictionnaire de théologie catholique* as "des opuscules de circonstance auxquels ont été adjointes quelques lettres dogmatiques.[52] One of these "opuscules" that he lists is *Confessio christianae fidei et ejusdem collatio cum papisticis haeresibus*.

This work of de Bèze, written in French for his father, Pierre de Bèze, in 1556, was revised and translated into Latin in 1560 and began to enjoy considerable popularity as a clear expression of Reformed doctrine. It is shorter than the *Institutes* of Calvin but more developed than Calvin's *Petit*

---

51.   *Ibid.*, p. 141.

52.   Dublanchy, E. *D.T.C.*, II. Col. 811.

catéchisme or other particular confessions written as occasional pieces by de Bèze. He himself explained why he wrote this *Confession* in the preface of the French edition of 1559:

> ...the duty of a true Christian is to have ready and at hand some summary and resolution of the principal points of religion and of the principal reasons by which he can both strengthen himself in them and be able to resist enemies of truth, according to his vocation, and to communicate his spiritual riches. Therefore, being requested to render an account of my faith by someone to whom, after God, I most owe obedience, I have just prepared this summary, which I have entitled *Confession of Faith*, in which I have gathered in the best order that I could that which I have learned in Christian religion by reading the Old and New Testaments with the aid of the most faithful expositors.[53]

After listing this work and the others which enter into the category of "Ouvrages de théologie systématique," Dublanchy concludes this section in writing the following:

> Dans toutes ses productions théologiques, de Bèze se montre toujours fidèle disciple de Calvin dont il réproduit toutes les conceptions dogmatiques, particulièrement sur le prédestinatianisme le péché rigide, sur le péche originel, la déstruction du libre arbitre et la justification réellement inadmissible.[54]

Bossuet, Bishop of Meaux, testifies to the use of Calvin's teaching in the subsequent presentation by de Bèze of various doctrines.[55] In his *Biographie universelle*, Michaud declares that de Bèze at the Colloque de Poissy "qui y joua un des principaux rôles, fut plutôt rhéteur que théolgien."[56] But we shall present in more detail the eucharistic teachings of de Bèze at Poissy in our subsequent chapter.

At a first glance we recognize in the *Confession* a comparable structure to that of the *Institution*. Of course, it is not nearly so long and

---

53.   Raitt, Jill. *The Eucharistic Theology of Theodore Beza: Development of the Reformed Doctrine*. (Atlanta: Scholars Press, 1972) pp. 11-12.

54.   Dublanchy, E. *D.T.C.*, II. Col. 811.

55.   Bossuet, Jacques Bénigne. *Histoire des Variations des églises protestantes*. (Paris: Desprez, 1691) t.4.

56.   Michaud, Mm. *Biographie universelle*. (Paris: Vivès, 1880) Vol. 4, col. 259.

detailed. Peculiar to de Bèze is that he begins this exposition with the importance of the "Word" within the Reformed Church. This would seem to indicate the concurrence of his own personal, ministerial experience with that of the Reformed Church. Both authors deal with the sacraments *in genere* before entering into a study of the Eucharist itself. De Bèze reveals, however, in this first redaction a more organized and "scholastic" approach to his presentation. Much has already been written about the influence of the academic experience that he had as a professor of classics at Lausanne over a period of ten years.[57] Despite this difference in style, de Bèze does follow Calvin's ideas meticulously. In Book IV, ch. 14 Calvin presents a doctrine of the sacraments *in genere*. He teaches that a "sacrament is an outward sign by which the Lord seals on our consciences the promises of his good will toward us in order to sustain the weakness of our faith; and we in turn attest our piety toward him in the presence of the Lord and of his angels and before men."[58] Calvin, after this initial definition, has recourse to St. Augustine's definition of a sacrament as a "visible sign of a sacred thing" or "a visible form of an invisible grace."[59]

In Article XXXI of the *Confession* de Bèze writes:

...ce que nous appelons sacrement en ce présent traité, ce sont certains signes, des marques ou des témoignages visibles ordonnés de Dieu pour l'usage continuel de toute son Eglise pendant qu'elle est en ce pélerinage terrien.[60]

Here we note that de Bèze remains faithful to Calvin even to the point of using the technical, theological word "signe." He develops this notion as does Calvin. But even more importantly, de Bèze uses St. Augustine as his *argumentum ex auctoritate* as did his predecessor. We know

---

57.　Geisendorf, Paul-F. *Théodore de Bèze* (Genève: Jullien, 1967) pp. 33ff.

58.　McNeill, John T. *Calvin: Institutes of the Christian Religion.* (Philadelphia: Westminster, 1960) p. 1277.

59.　St. Augustine. *De cathechisandis rudibus,* XXVI.

60.　Reveillaud, Michel. "La Confession de foi du chrétien," *La revue réformee,* Nos. 23-24, 1955, pp. 67-68.

the importance of St. Augustine would be equally so for Théodore de Bèze as he had been for Calvin himself.

At the outset of Calvin's treatment of the Holy Supper in the *Institutions*, he begins on a practical note with the section entitled "Signification et utilité de la Sainte Cène." Given the desire of Calvin to teach a fundamental doctrine for all his followers, his pragmatic approach is understandable. In contrast, de Bèze is more precise, briefer and more scholastic. Then Calvin presents a rather wordy section on "Matter and sign to be distinguished."[61] On the other hand, de Bèze approaches his treatment of the sacraments very methodically. After stating that there are only two sacraments in the Christian Church, he proceeds directly to outline the four points under which he will develop his thesis in Article XXXVII:

> Le premier concerne les signes, ce qu'ils sont et en quel sens on les nomme 'signes.' Le second concerne ce qui est signifié par eux. Le troisième concerne la conjonction des signes et de la réalité signifiée. Le quatrième concerne la manière par laquelle on participe tant aux signes qu'à la réalité signifiée.[62]

Without entering into a careful analysis here of this teaching, we realize the likeness of the presentations of our two Reformers at the same time that we become aware of some differences both in content and in form.

Following their respective introductions, each of our authors directly proceeds to show how baptism satisfies the notion of "sacrament" as they have presented it.

The two theologians then pass directly from their consideration of baptism to the sacrament of the Holy Supper. In our preceding analysis of the *De Coena Domini* we have tried to analyze those teachings of Calvin contained in both the *Institutes* and in the *Petit traité de la Cène*. This was the teaching that was to take seed in de Bèze and served as the point of departure for his eucharistic doctrine.

Having stated the importance of St. Augustine for Calvin and for de Bèze and aware of a scholastic influence on both these Reformers, we note a

61.   McNeill, J. p. 1290-1291.

62.   Reveillaud, M. pp. 74-75.

remarkable parallel between them and St. Thomas Aquinas. However, we have found no serious previous book or article on this point.

In the area that concerns us here, Calvin appears to use much of the material presented in the *Contra Gentiles* of St. Thomas. Book IV, Articles LVI, LVII and LVIII treat the notion of the necessity of the sacraments, their distinctions under the Old and New Law and finally their number. Thomas then proceeds to the study of baptism and subsequently the Eucharist. This is also Calvin's procedure.

In contrast, Théodore de Bèze clearly uses not the *Contra Gentiles*, which is an earlier and less precise work of Thomas, but rather, he seems to follow another Thomistic source: namely, the *Summa Theologica*. I find no mention of this in any of the latest scholarly work by Olivier Fatio at the University of Geneva. However, Dr. Jill Raitt, professor of religious studies at the University of Missouri, points out that "Bèza's sacramental teaching comes so close" to that of St. Thomas in the IIIa Pars, Question 62 that it contains Aquinas' doctrine concerning principal and instrumental causality and declares the sign-cause nature of the sacraments of the New Law which effect what they signify, "*efficiunt quod figurant.*"[63]

A concise notion of the "closeness" of doctrines of de Bèze in the *Confession* and of St. Thomas in the *Summa*, can be presented by a diagram showing the correspondence between the question posed and considered by the Angelic Doctor and the Reformer.

---

63. Raitt, J. p. 18, note 39.

The pagination of the latter refers to that of Reveillaud's edition:

SUBJECT	CONFESSION (Page)	SUMMA[64] (Question)
Essence & Nature	12	60
Sign	23,30	60, a.18
Necessity	34	61
Grace	3,4	62
Character	29	63
Cause	21	64
Ministers	38	64, a.4,10
Number	15	65

This table is intended simply to show there may be an influence at play on de Bèze that was not present on Calvin at an earlier period. Of course, Calvin presented his doctrine of the Eucharist in the much broader context in Book IV of the *Institutions*. However, even in his *De Coena Domini*, we do see St. Augustine influencing his thought. But St. Thomas Aquinas is not so clearly present to his writing as the above table suggests quite clearly in regard to Théodore de Bèze in his *Confession de foi du chrétien*. They were two different men. If, as we have tried to show, de Bèze was very faithful to Calvin, he still was an intellectual with his own creativity and abilities. He seems to have made use of these qualities in writing poetry and drama as well as the more polemical commentaries on Sacred Scriptures, etc. that understandably occupied him more once he became the leader of the Reformed movement at Geneva.

We are now going to consider the work of another leader of his Church, namely, Francis de Sales. This Bishop of Geneva, displaced to Annecy in Savoy because of the Reformers' presence, was also a prolific writer. This Protestant and this Catholic leader met on three occasions. But before considering those meetings, we should like to present the eucharistic doctrine of St. Francis de Sales. Francis was very faithful to the Council of Trent. We know that this Council was convened in order to deal with the

---

64. *Summa Theologica*. IIIa Pars.

reformation movement that was having such a major influence on the Roman Church. Bishop, author and spiritual writer, Francis de Sales reflects the 17th-century's Catholic reaction to the Reformation. We shall present only his doctrine of the Eucharist in attempting to appreciate one element in the fundamental differences that existed between the Reformation Churches and the Roman Catholic Church immediately following the closing of the Council of Trent.

François de Sales à 51 ans (1618). Auteur inconnu. Visitation de Turin.
(L'auréole a été ajoutée après la canonisation)

CHAPTER II

François de Sales

Francis de Sales is more a spiritual author than he is a methodical theologian. To understand his theology of the Eucharist, we must understand his concept of the Church. For him the Church enlightened by the Holy Spirit makes us discover:

> le bel or de la sainte dilection, qui se fait excellemment entrevoir, dorant de son lustre incomparable toute la science des Saintz et la rehaussant au-dessus de toute science.[1]

dilection which is no other than the love of God:

> Tout est a l'amour, en l'amour, pour l'amour et d'amour en la sainte Eglise,[2]

a love through which we have received the revelation of God and which still remains a mystery.

> Mays comme nous sçavons bien que toute la clarté du jour provient du soleil, et disons neanmoins pour l'ordinaire que le soleil n'esclaire pas sinon, quand a descouvert, il darde ses rayons en quelque endroit, de mesme, bien que toute la doctrine chrestienne soit de l'amour sacré, si est-ce que nous n'honnorons pas indistinctement toute la théologie du tiltre de ce divin amour, ains seulement les parties d'icelle qui contemplent l'origine, la nature, les propriétés et les operations d'iceluy en particulier.[3]

---

1. *Oeuvres*. Edition complète. Annecy, Niérat, 1892-1964, IV, p. 4.

2. *Ibid.*, Thanks to J.-L. Leroux for his important inspiration in Ch. II.

3. *Ibid.*

32

Theology does not always study the mystery of God Himself. There are other ways to seek to understand and love Him.

Francis de Sales proposes one of them where it involves the Eucharist. It is not original. Rather it is that of a pastor. He seeks to nourish those who aspire to live by the Gospel which conveys a concept of the human existence based on love.

Thus this love of God is the very foundation stone of Salesian theology. Scripture and tradition are the building blocks. It is within this concept that Francis' theology of the Eucharist is revealed. How do these foundations influence the Salesian Eucharistic theology?

A.   *THEOLOGICAL FOUNDATIONS*

   1.   Love:

We see in the preface of the *Traité de l'Amour de Dieu* that Salesian theology seeks to know about the infinite character, the absolute love and the goodness of that which

> c'est le propre de la bonté de se communiquer car de soy mesme elle est communicative.[4]

This communication of goodness is exercised at two levels. One is God Himself and this is the mystery of the Trinity. Outside of God it is the reality of creation. In this way the love of God becomes the cause of creation, of the incarnation and of the redemption. Thus man is created by love and for love.[5]

   2.   The heart:

Salesian theology is "affectif." It wants the heart involved in the devotion that is expressed. Francis describes himself to Saint Jeanne de Chantal as a profoundly loving man:

> il n'y a point d'ames au monde, comme je pense, qui cherissent plus cordialement, tendrement et, pour le dire tout a la bonne foy, plus amoureusement que moy; car il a pleu a Dieu de faire mon coeur ainsy.[6]

---

4.   *Ibid.*, X, pp. 312-313.

5.   *Ibid.*, IV, pp. 95-102.

6.   *Ibid.*, XX, p. 216.

Hence, the object of theology as Francis envisages it is the God of love, who causes man, the loving creature, to be discovered and to be drawn naturally to Him. The 16th- and 17th-century humanistic movement has its effect on Francis. He seeks to bring out the relationships of man with God. Man is not to wonder if God exists. God's existence is a condition *sine qua non* of Francis' thought. What does predominate in his theology, however, is man's autonomy in relation to God. In other words, it is the major question of liberty and grace. Francis has great trust in human reason and in man's basic tendency towards God. For this reason he writes:

> L'homme est la perfection de l'univers, l'esprit est la perfection de l'homme, l'amour celle de l'esprit, et la charité celle de l'amour: c'est pourquoy l'amour de Dieu est la fin, la perfection et l'excellence de l'univers.[7]

This relationship of liberty and grace anchors in Francis the conviction that the only way to live this is by an authentic charity which reconciles human liberty with the divine will. The cement of this union is Christ.

3.   Christ:

Man has been created for God and this is revealed to us by the Incarnation of his Son. There is a relationship established between God and man which is a:

> convenance grande, mais secrette; convenance que chacun connoist, et que peu de gens entendent, convenance qu'on ne peut nier, mais qu'on ne peut bien penetrer.[8]

For Francis, then, the complete humanity of His Son was necessary in order that God communicate all His love to us. This revelation distinguishes the Christian from other believers. Francis, in a transport of joy, speaks of this union:

> ce noeud indussoluble avec lequel l'humanité est jointe et unie avec la Divinité, cette oeuvre incomparable de l'Incarnation en laquelle Dieu s'est fait homme et l'homme est fait Dieu.[9]

---

7.   *Ibid.*, V, p. 165.

8.   *Ibid.*, IV, p. 74.

9.   *Ibid.*, IX, p. 117.

The key then of Salesian theology is Jesus Christ, true God and true man. Francis' theology is founded on the profound and loving knowledge of the divinity of the person of Jesus, whose historical and mystical reality serves as the principle and the end of man's existence. Man contemplates this historical reality within creation. He becomes aware of the mystical reality in his personal experience of Jesus Christ. This makes man realize that God wishes to be united with us. Francis writes:

> le grand Sauveur fut le premier en l'intention divine et en ce projet eternel que la divine Providence fit de la production des creatures: et en contemplation de ce fruict desirable fut plantee la vigne de l'univers et établie la succession de plusieurs generations, qui, a guise de feuilles et de fleurs, le devoyent preceder.[10]

Salesian theology leads us to a Christocentric conception of creation. All creation is an act of love, tending towards Christ, the effect of the love and the goodness of God who sought only to give Himself to creation and to draw that creation to Himself in a union with the Man-God, the first born of all creation.

4. The Church:

It is on this faith in Jesus Christ, the center of our Christian life that the Church has been founded. And it is the Church which today continues with the Spirit, the loving regeneration of the creation already saved by Jesus Christ. Confronted with Reformist thought, Francis affirms this essential mission of the Church. This mission in his theology has been received from Christ and transmitted by the apostles:

> Christus rogavit pro Petro ut non deficeret fides ejus; Luc 22. C'est le chef de l'Eglise qui est la colomne et le firmament de la verité, comme dit saint Pol a son Timothee.[11]

Many spiritual writers consider Salesian theology as an expression of the living faith and tradition of the Church. Faithful to the concepts of the Church of the 17th century, Francis thinks that there is only one true

---

10.   *Ibid.*, IV, p. 103.

11.   *Ibid.*, VII, pp. 50-51.

theology, that of fidelity to the teachings of Christ retained by the apostolic tradition and transmitted to us in the Church:

> Ne regardons jamais les cogitations de la foy qui ne sont pas de Dieu ny fondëes sur la pierre de l'Eglise Catholique; mays brisons les, et rompons leurs pointes contre ceste pierre.[12]

B.   *PASTOR-THEOLOGIAN*

These four buildings stones - love, heart, Christ, Church - are going to support the action and the thought of Francis de Sales during the time of the Catholic reformation in the 16th and 17th centuries. In the very territory of the Reformation, Francis will act as missionary in the Chablais and as Bishop of Geneva. It is in the light of his action in these circumstances that we shall try to outline his perception of the Eucharist.

1.   His juridicial and theological formation as well as the ecclesial and political institutions of his time do not produce an innovative theology. He is not a revolutionary. All his life he will be faithful to the pope, the Church and his Duke.

2.   He will seek the interior reformation of the Church. The thought of important Catholic reformers such as Theresa of Avila and Phillippe Neri influenced him profoundly.

3.   It is at this level that we can call Francis de Sales the "doux apôtre de l'amour." His action is not based on a classical theology which is based on a theory of knowledge and harmonized with the revealed truths. Rather does his theology begin with the mystery itself of love and manifests the marriage between the human and the divine nature. The unifying principle, the cause and the end of every union is in the person of Jesus Christ. This union is one of love. Thus it is free and existentially engages the whole human person. It is begun and is active in the Church and particularly in the sacrament when the matter is changed by Christ into his Mystical Body in order that he may live in our very freedom.

4.   Both his "political" and "theological" concepts joined with his fidelity to the living faith of the Church, are what constitutes Francis' understanding.

---

12.   *Ibid.*, p. 52.

5. The sacrament of the Body and the Blood of Jesus Christ is the greatest sign of the eternal and infinite love of God for us:

> Vrayment ceste creance du tressaint Sacrement, qui contient en verité, realité et substance le vray et naturel Cors de Nostre Seigneur est vrayement l'abbregé de nostre foy.[13]

In this simple affirmation is contained the whole doctrine of the Eucharist for St. Francis de Sales. It is in the reaffirmation of the Council of Trent that he will develop his "affective" theology of the Eucharist and with which he will confront the teachings of Luther and Calvin.

For Francis the doctrinal decisions of the Council of Trent were ultimately authoritative because they were the Church's decisions. They will be his positions. However, we must always keep in mind that his theological treatment arises from his humanistic and theological erudition; in a way analogous to that of both Calvin and Théodore de Bèze. They are all men of their times. However, in Francis de Sales, we find no theological treatise as a unit such as we find in Calvin and in de Bèze. Rather shall we find throughout his writings a doctrine which embraces simultaneously creation and humanity as they are included in the love of the Father for Christ and for His Church.

The principal Salesian writings on the Eucharist are found in the priestly and missionary period of St. Francis de Sales. Francis has just finished his studies at the University of Padua in 1592. He then returns to Savoy and is made provost of the diocese of Annecy. On December 18, 1593 Francis is ordained a priest by Bishop de Granier. Upon his own request, he then goes to the region of the Chablais. The object of his mission is to bring back to the Roman church the former Catholics of this region who have been won over to Calvinism. Faced with this Protestant heresy, Francis will reaffirm the traditional positions of the Catholic Church's doctrines. He will accomplish this through his preaching and the very manner of living his life. Once he is consecrated bishop, in 1602, his writings on the Eucharist will become less numerous. We find these Eucharistic writings particularly in his sermons and his letters in which he is actually giving spiritual direction.

---

13.   *Ibid.*, I, p. 338.

Certain doctrinal affirmations or allusions to Holy Communion or the celebration of the Eucharist are naturally in these documents. However, he discusses or develops the treatment of other subjects of all kinds. The two principal works which date from his years as a bishop, and in which we discover his "affective" theology are:

      a.   *L'introduction à la vie dévote* published in Lyon in 1608 for the first edition. In this book Francis offers to all men, whatever might be their condition in life, the possibility of knowing God and of living as Christians.

      b.   *Le traité de l'amour de Dieu* also published in Lyon but eight years later in 1616. In this treatise on the theology of "affective" love, Francis depicts the Christian so penetrated with divine charity that he seeks to transmit it to his fellow Christians. The style, the number of images, the beauty of the language make of it a magnificent poem of love.

Besides these two major works, there are the following:

1.   Eucharistic writings from the missionary period (1593-1602):

      a.   Sermons:

          1)   Summary of a sermon on the Blessed Sacrament: June 9-16, 1594, (VII, p. 182).

          2)   Summary of a sermon on the Blessed Sacrament: 1594, (X, p. 434).

          3)   Summary of a sermon on transubstantiation and the sacrifice of the Mass: October, 1594, (VII, p. 223).

          4)   Summary of a sermon on the Blessed Eucharist prefigured in the Old Testament: September 17, 1595, (VII, p. 268).

          5)   Notes for a sermon on the real presence of Our Lord in the Eucharist: April 13, 1596, (VII, p. 287).

          6)   Sermon for the Feast of Corpus Christi: June 13, 1596, (VII, p. 289).

          7)   Summary of a sermon for the Sunday within the Octave of Corpus Christi: June 16, 1596, (VII, p. 297).

8)   Fragment of a sermon for the day of the Octave of Corpus Christi: June 20, 1596, (VII, p. 301).

9)   Notes for a sermon on the Holy Eucharist: 1596, (VII, p. 303).

10) Dogmatic sermon on the Holy Eucharist: July, 1597, (VII, p. 321).

11) Second sermon on the same subject: July, 1597, (VII, p. 328).

12) Third sermon on the same subject: July, 1597, (VII, p. 342).

b.   Short treatises:

13) Conferences: Short "apologetic" papers concerning the Catholic doctrine and distributed by Francis to the inhabitants of the Chablais from January, 1595 to June 1596:

   a)   "Que l'analogie de la Foy ne peut servir de règle aux Ministres pour establir leur doctrine": (I, p. 336). Part II. Chap. 8, Art. III.

   b)   Des Sacrements: (I, p. 336). Part III, Chap. 1.

14) Codex Fabrianus: Written between 1595 and 1605 and published in 1606: (XXIII, p. 67-241).

c.   Other writings:

15) Poetry. In honor of the Blessed Sacrament: August 6-15, 1598, (XXII, p. 107).

2.   Eucharistic writings of the episcopal or pastoral period: (1602-1622):

a.   Sermons:

16) Plan of a sermon on Holy Communion: 1604, (VIII, p. 12).

17) Plan of a sermon for a Feast of the Ascension: May 24, 1604, (VIII, p. 20).

b.   Works:

    18)   Introduction to the Devout Life: 1608:

        a)   The Holy Mass and how to assist: (III, p. 100).

        b)   Frequent Communion: (III, p. 116).

        c)   How to receive Holy Communion: (III, p. 120).

c.   Another writing:

    19)   Note on the real presence of Our Lord Jesus Christ in the Eucharist: 1619, (XXIII, p. 244).

3.   The "lost" writings on the Eucharist:

A part of the writings of Francis on the Eucharist are not now available to us. There were sermons on the Eucharistic doctrine that were preached to the upper classes of the Chablais. It was in the autumn of 1595 at Thonon that Francis gave these sermons. We know of them through a letter that he wrote to his friend, Antoine Favre, in which he expressed his joy at having been able to attract Calvinists in speaking on the subject of the Eucharist:

> Voici enfin, mon Frère, qu'une porte plus large et plus belle s'ouvre à nous pour entrer dans cette moisson de Chrétiens, car il s'en fallut peu hier que M. d'Avully et les syndics de la ville, comme on les appelle, ne vinssent ouvertement à la prédication, parce qu'ils avaient ouï dire que je devais parler du très auguste Sacrement de l'autel.[14]

We possess only the plan of this sermon.[15] However, we know that it was followed by many others as he points out subsequently in his letter:

> J'ai promis qu'à la prédication suivante je mettrais, par les Ecritures, ce dogme en plus grande lumière...[16]

So Francis wrote a series of sermons which were addressed to people of Thonon, but which apparently no longer exist. The same thing is true for

---

14.   *Ibid.*, XI, p. 158.

15.   *Ibid.*, VII, p. 269.

16.   *Ibid.*, XI, p. 158.

the "placards" from the *Controversies*. Francis had written on the Eucharist there as well. He writes:

> Je me reserve sur ce sujet (le Corps et le Sang du Christ) quand nous traitterons de la sainte Messe.[17]

Even if we do not have these various writings, we do have the plan for the sermons that he gave in Thonon. This plan is given in the first sermon that we have cited above.[18] To counter the Protestants' theories, Francis wants to prove the "raysons de l'Eglise" and he demonstrated these in six points:

> Car, je le preuveray
> 1.   par les figures et praedictions;
> 2.   par la promesse qu'en a faict Nostre Seigneur en saint Jan, 6; 3.
> 3.   par l'institution du Saint Sacrement;
> 4.   par des autres passages, par l'antiquité et les miracles et les raysons, et toute sorte de tesmoins.   Cinquiesmement, je monstreray que ce Sacrement est non suelement Sacrement mays Sacrifice; Sixiesmement, je monstreray la convenance, et respondray aux raysons contrayres, et iray poursuyvant selon que Dieu me donnera les moyens.[19]

Only the first point is considered in the sermon's plan that we possess.

Francis' method seems simple to us. What does Holy Scripture say about this subject? How have the Fathers and the apostolic and Church tradition interpreted the Scripture? What can ancient philosophy, miracles and reasons tell us? In other words, what argumentation and demonstration are we able to draw from "l'Escriture, la rayson et la vraye théologie."[20]

At this point we can state that the thought of Francis on the Eucharist is formed by his knowledge of scripture, theology and philosophy. Though not an original theologian, he shows a solid acquisition and assimilation of this doctrine. Now it is our task to take out of his writing his thought on the Eucharist itself.

---

17.   *Ibid.*, I, p. 356.

18.   *Ibid.*, VII, p. 269.

19.   *Ibid.*

20.   *Ibid.*, VII, p. 270.

We shall begin this brief study of the Eucharist in Salesian theology by a few reflections on the eucharistic rite. A liturgical offering, this is an act of grace containing the mystery itself of love in its work of union, of reunion and of pedagogy in the mystery of the Church. The realization of this mystery among us is brought about through a rite of the Church.

C.   EUCHARIST AND LITURGY

Francis attaches great importance to the liturgical action, and more particularly the eucharistic liturgy, whose importance is underlined by the Council of Trent to which he is faithful.

Liturgy is the act which raises praise to the heavenly Father. It must reflect the harmony that exists between God and man. Thus the insistence by Francis on the *beau*, the good order of the liturgical acts, the care and the maintenance of the places of worship and of liturgical objects.

The Council of Trent had rendered the liturgy of the Eucharist very "clerical." However, Francis along with other notable Catholic Reformers, encourages a new "popular" eucharistic liturgy. This popular liturgy takes such forms as the procession of the Blessed Sacrament and the Forty Hours devotion such as that which was held in Thonon in 1598 to celebrate the conversion of the Chablais to Catholicism. The "confrèries de pénitents" represent another form of popular eucharistic devotion.

Two emphases of Salesian liturgy are:

a.   Tradition:

The liturgy is the expression of the faith of Christians in the Church. Francis insists of his priests that they live the liturgy in the manner taught by the council of Trent:

> Tous ecclesiastiques suyvront en tout et par tout les decretz du tressaint Concile de Trente et specialement en ce qui est de l'Office divin et celebration de la Messe.[21]

At this moment in the historical evolution of the Church, Francis proposes, not another explanation of the liturgical act, but rather a new expression of this liturgy in a language which could be understood by all believers. His

---

21.   *Ibid.*, XXIII, pp. 266-267.

"affectif" language, coming from man's heart, will have the desired resonance. The presentation of the Mass, as contained in the *Introduction à la vie dévote*, helps us to see the "affectif" movement which translates for the Bishop of Geneva both the doctrine of the Church in all its specificity as well as the dynamism of the encounter between God and man:

> Je ne vous ay encor point parlé du soleil des exercices spirituelz, qui est le tressaint, sacré et tressouverain Sacrifice et Sacrement de la Messe, centre de la religion chrestienne, coeur de la devotion, ame de la piete, mystere ineffable qui comprend l'abisme de la charité divine, et par lequel Dieu s'appliquant reellement a nous, nous communique magnifiquement ses graces et faveurs.[22]

Francis then teaches this profound Eucharistic doctrine while at the same time speaking of the Eucharist as a daily act and invites each Christian to participate in it as often as possible.[23]

      b.   The living reality of the presence of Christ:

This is essential in Francis' teaching on the Eucharist. He encourages Philothea to encounter Christ Himself. He invites her during Mass to be part of the life of Our Lord, to participate in his death and resurrection, since the Eucharistic sacrifice, in its liturgical form, is the memorial of the gift of God to men; that is, His only Son.[24] This is shown in a letter to Jeanne de Chantal, where he underlines the union of humanity itself with Christ in the Eucharist:

> Ah! ce dis-je, o Sauveur de nostre coeur, puisque meshuy nous serons tous les jours a vostre table pour manger non seulement vostre pain, mays vous mesme, qui estes notre pain vivant et suressentiel, faites que tous les jours nous facions une bonne et parfaite digestion de cette viande tres parffaitte, et que nous vivions perpetuellement embausmés de vostre sacree douceur, bonté et amour.[25]

The Eucharistic liturgy then unites us to Christ:

---

22.   *Ibid.*, III, p. 100.

23.   *Ibid.*, III, p. 101.

24.   *Ibid.*, III, pp. 101-102.

25.   *Ibid.*, XIV, pp. 374-375.

Qui reçoit la tressaint Communion, il reçoit Jésus-Christ vivant.[26]

This union then is of each Christian with Christ but also the union of Christ with this Church in this public liturgical act, the fundamental and sacramental rite of the Christian faith.

Without developing fully this notion of rite in St. Francis, we may say that he is faithful to what the Church regards as the structure of this rite: that is, the priest and the Mass. It is with the priest that Christians profess the resurrection of Jesus Christ in offering:

avec le prestre le sacrifice de vostre Redempteur a Dieu son Pere pour vous et pour toute l'Eglise.[27]

The second, the Mass, which is the sacred action itself, has its origin in the pascal mystery. This pascal mystery is the foundation of the eucharistic rite in its symbolic reality. It is at the pascal meal that:

le Sauveur ne voulant prononcer son testament qu'en la croix et un peu avant que de mourir, appliqua neanmoins son sceau et cachetta son testament avant toutes autres choses.....Il appliqua ce sceau sacré lors qu'il institua le tres saint et tres adorable Sacrement de l'autel, qu'il appelle son nouveau testament; Sacrement qui contient en soy la Divinité et l'humanité tout ensemble, et entierement la Personne sacrée de Nostre Seigneur.[28]

For Francis, the Mass is the expression of God's loving plan for humanity in the Incarnation and Redemption of his Son. It is in and by the Eucharist that we manifest our participation in this plan. We participate then:

En la Messe, il y a 5 parties: prieres, ceremonies et consecration, oblation et communication. Les deux premieres sont pour reverence et dont nous n'avons pas expres commandement en particulier.[29]

Communion, which for Francis is both oblation and communication, is our participation in this divine life in this world; it is also in view of our

---

26.   *Ibid.*, XVII, p. 221.

27.   *Ibid.*, III, p. 101.

28.   *Ibid.*, IX, p. 271.

29.   *Ibid.*, VII, p. 229.

44

definitive union with Christ in eternal life. This point, too long to develop here, is advanced at greater length in the *Introduction*.[30]

Finally, the third essential element in Francis' conception of the eucharistic rite is the priest. His concept of the Eucharist involves the priest as a condition *sine qua non* of the Church's eucharistic liturgy. He conceives of the priest as the one who is to teach the believer to speak with God. This is done in Francis' notion by his revealing to the faithful the tenderness of God for him who believes. Hence, the Eucharist must be the center of the life of the priest. All his preaching, in word and in act, must be founded on the Mystery itself of God and thus a mystery of love. Every word of the priest must be motivated and inspired as much by his love of the truth as by the truth of his love. These gifts become the priest's through the Mass. Francis teaches this in a passage in which he reveals what was possible for him and which he is sure is possible for other priests:

> Ayant receu la sainte Eucharistie de la main du Souverain Pontife, le jour de l'Annonciation, mon ame fut fort consolee interieurement; et Dieu me fit la grace de me donner de grandes lumieres sur le mistere de l'Incarnation, me faisant connoistre d'une maniere inexplicable comme le Verbe prit un cors, par la puissance du Pere et par l'operation du Saint Esprit, dans le chaste sein de Marie, le voulant bien luy mesme pour habiter parmy nous, des qu'il seroit homme comme nous. Cest Homme Dieu m'a aussi donné une connoissance eslevee et savoureuse sur la Transsubstantiation, sur son entree en mon ame et sur le ministere des Pasteurs de l'Eglise.[31]

Francis cannot conceive of the Eucharist without its being confected by the priest ordained by the Church to that end.

D.   *EUCHARIST AS WORD IN ACT*

The presence of God is in the Eucharist, in His Word made flesh. This principle involves creation and that fullness provided for it by the Eucharist:

> Je suis bien ayse qu'en vostre ruche et au milieu de cet essaim nouveau, vous ayes vostre Roy, vostre miel et vostre Tout. La presence de cette sacree Humanité remplira toute vostre

---

30.   *Ibid.*, III, pp. 101-102.

31.   *Ibid.*, XXII, p. 110.

mayson de suavité, et c'est une grande consolation aux ames qui sont attentives a la foy d'avoir ce thresor de vie proche.[32]

God becomes present in bread and wine. He wants to become present in us to the same degree that he is in the offerings. He counteracts our liberties and the immaturity of our hearts. This intentionality of the Eucharist is a constant theme in the letters and in the direction of St. Francis:

> Imaginés-vous que comme l'abeille ayant recueilli sur les fleurs la rosee du ciel et le suc plus exquis de la terre, et l'ayant reduit en miel, le porte dans sa ruche, ainsi le prestre ayant pris sur l'autel le Sauveur du monde, vray Filz de Dieu, qui comme une rosee est descendu du Ciel, et vrai Filz de la Vierge, qui comme fleur est sorti de la terre de nostre humanité, il le met en viande de suavité dedans vostre bouche.[33]

This divine presence seeks to be a cosmic presence: we contemplate in the Eucharist the God who transforms, who changes, who converts completely. God, present in the universe, seeks to be recognized as this transformer and forces man to perceive Him in matter. The Christian no longer sees with limited vision, but the word of Christ by the word of the priest transforms his vision: "This bread is Christ".

a. This Eucharist then is truly a word in act and thus becomes a sacrament. As all sacraments, the Eucharist has its origin and its efficacy in the passion of Christ.

> Le costé du Sauveur, percé par la lance sur la Croix, fut la vive source de toutes les graces dont les ames sont arrousees par les saintz Sacremens.[34]

Commemorating the passion itself, the Eucharist is the greatest of the sacraments:

> Après la Résurrection, il (le Christ) voulut garder de cette passion le plus éclatant souvenir, tant dans l'Eglise militante que dans l'Eglise triomphante: ici-bas dans l'Eucharistie.[35]

---

32. *Ibid.*, XVI, p. 313.

33. *Ibid.*, III, p. 121.

34. *Ibid.*, II, p. 246.

35. *Ibid.*, VIII, p. 292.

46

These sacraments have their beginning in the love of God that we know by the Incarnation and the Redemption. They are simply:

> des canaux par lesquels, pour ainsi parler, Dieu descend à nous.[36]

Their effects are:

> divers, quoy qu'ils n'ayent tous qu'une mesme fin et pretention, qui est de nous unir à Dieu.[37]

They continue the redeeming Incarnation whose goal is to bring us to a participation in the divine nature. The Word of God, by the sacraments, has the power to give us eternal life. Francis writes the following to bring out this idea:

> Par la vertu de la parole de Dieu. Alors nous verrons cet admirable miracle de la transsubstantiation qui s'opere tous les jours au Sacrement de l'Eucharistie; car en cette resurrection generale se fera la transsubstantiation des cendres qui estoyent dans les tombeaux ou ailleurs, en vrays corps vivans.[38]

Thus is our life transformed. We are no longer "profane" since we are created to participate in the divine life; however, the sacraments are efficacious only under the condition that we are disposed to accept in faith that which they transmit to us; that is, all that Christ has promised us in his alliance with us. Francis in the garden at the Gallery, says to his Visitandines:

> Faisons donc de nostre costé ce qui est de nostre pouvoir pour nous bien preparer à recevoir ce Pain supersubstantiel, nous abandonnant totalement à la divine Providence...; et nous asseurons que Nostre Seigneur accomplira de son costé la promesse qu'il nous a faite de nous transformer en luy, eslevant nostre bassesse jusque à estre unie avec sa grandeur.[39]

Love does not suffer violence; it is given and received freely. The sacraments, given out of love, must be received with love and by love. For the Eucharist, which is the center of our Christian life, this is especially true:

---

36. *Ibid.*, VI, p. 337.

37. *Ibid.*

38. *Ibid.*, X, p. 315.

39. *Ibid.*, VI, p. 341.

O saint et parfaict memorial de l'Evangile, o admirable receuil de nostre foy: ...quill puysse...o Seigneur, croire a vostre praesence en ce tressaint Sacrement, comme presche vostre sainte Eglise, a recueilly et suce le doux miel de toutes les fleurs de vostre sainte Religion, a grand peyne qu'il puysse jamais mescroire...: mays celle [la chair] du Sauveur, qui est toujours garnie de l'Esprit vivifiant et de son Verbe, je dis qu'elle proufite a tous ceux qui la reçoivent dignement pour la vie aeternelle.[40]

The Eucharist is surely the greatest sign of God's infinite and eternal love of us. It is at the very heart of the life of the Church. In it, everything is drawn together, everything is taken up again and raised to its true dimension which is divine and eternal:

Bonheur infini, Theotime, et lequel ne nous a pas seulement esté promis, mais nous en avons des arres au tressaint Sacrement de l'Eucharistie, festin perpetuel de la grace divine; car en iceluy nous recevons le sang du Sauveur en sa chair et sa chair en son sang, son sang nous estant appliqué par sa chair, sa substance par sa substance, a nostre propre bouche corporelle, affin que nous sachions qu'ainsy nous appliquera-il son essence divine au festin eternel de la gloire.[41]

Thus the Eucharist truly is the sacrament of the presence of the risen Christ, assembling in the same unique act the past, the present and the future: Christ is the same yesterday, today and tomorrow.

b.   The Eucharist is a sacramental act which has both form and matter. The words of institution constitute the form of the sacrament of the Eucharist. These were pronounced by Jesus Himself.[42] The Protestants did not dispute that the words of institution were the form of the Lord's Supper. However, they insisted that the words be repeated in the vernacular and be explained clearly. The words in the vernacular together with their explanation constitute "the form" for the Reformers. They use as their basis for this tenet the Gospel of Matthew: "Go forth therefore, to all the nations making of them disciples, baptizing them in the name of the Father and of the Son and of the Holy Spirit."[43] Referring to the Church, they use St.

---

40.   *Ibid.*, I, p. 339.

41.   *Ibid.*, IV, p. 202.

42.   *Ibid.*, XXIII, p. 93.

43.   Matthew, 28, 19.

Paul's letter to the Ephesians: "Christ wished to make it holy in purifying it with water which purifies by the Word."[44] For Francis, other passages contradict such an interpretation:

> Saint Pol enseigne aux Corinthiens comm'il faut celebrer la cene, mays on ny trouve point qu'il y soit commandé de precher; et affin que personne ne doutast que le rite qu'il proposoit fut legitime, il dict qu'il avoit ainsy apris de Nostre Seigneur.[45]

Francis sees the whole tradition of the Church as opposed to such an exegesis. The words of institution are the form of the sacrament of the Eucharist. It is not the discourse after the Last Supper as recounted by St. John that removes from the words of the institution their sacramental signification because:

> ce ne fut pas pour le mistere de la cene, qui estoit ja complet.[46]

The matter of the sacrament of the Eucharist is the bread and the wine become the body and the blood of the risen Christ by the action of the word itself of Jesus Christ.[47] The fact itself of calling the Eucharist "bread," that is, matter, object, is rejected by the Calvinists who cannot conceive of the presence of the risen Christ in it. Thus Francis objects to their position in the following way:

> Je réponds:
> 1.   que Paul emploie ce terme de pain, parce que Jésus-Christ l'avait aussi employé. Mais pour-quoi Jésus l'avait-il employé? Je réponds que le mot pain peut signifier des aliments d'espèces et de substances absolument différentes. C'est donc, d'après l'usage universel, un mot générique; il indique des choses qui se ressemblent par leur forme et leur destination plutôt que par la matière. De là: ceci est vraiment du pain. Dans le pain, en effet, il y a deux éléments; la matière et la forme; il n'est nullement nécessaire que la matière soit toujours la même...

---

44.   Ephesians, 5, 26.

45.   *Oeuvres*, I, p. 353.

46.   *Ibid.*, pp. 353-354.

47.   *Ibid.*, pp. 183-184.

2.   Une chose transformée garde souvent son premier nom:
Tu es poussière et tu retourneras en terre. Ainsi l'eau
changée en vin...

3.   De même très souvent, les Anges sont appelés hommes.
Donc, pour toutes ces causes, le mot pain est très
exact.[48]

Over and above the allegory used here by Francis, we can better understand the great importance given here to the matter, for Francis, creation is divinized by the Incarnation itself. From examples drawn from nature, his constant wonder before every created being, we become aware of this diametric refusal of the condemnation of our human body:

> Le Chretien doit aymer son corps comme une image vivante de celuy du Sauveur incarné, comme issu de mesme tige avec iceluy, et, par consequent, lui appartenant en parentage et consanguinite; sur tout apres que nous avons renouvellé l'alliance par la reception reele de ce divin Cors du Redempteur au tres adorable Sacrement de l'Eucharistie, et que, par le Baptesme, Confirmation et autres Sacremens, nous nous sommes dediés et consacrés a la souveraine Bonté.[49]

It is in this way that we profess our faith in the presence of the risen Christ; a faith which has been purified by baptism which is the door which introduces us into the community of Christ's faithful who are united to Him here below by the Eucharist.

A poem composed in honor of the Blessed Sacrament in August of 1598 while Francis was in the Chablais reveals a great deal of his theology of the Eucharist:

---

48.   *Ibid.*, pp. 299-300 (original text is in Latin).

49.   *Ibid.*, IV, pp. 192-193.

50

Nous confessons, o Seigneur Dieu
Que ton cors est (en) ce lieu.
Ta parole
N'est frivole
Ni ton Eglise aussi,
Laquelle le croit ainsy.

Nous admirons ta bonté
Adorans ta majesté
Qui, presente,
Se contente
En ces bas lieux se ranger
Pour mieux se faire manger.

O Pain caeleste et vivant,
Tout esprit t'aille adorant,
L'homme et l'Ange
Qui te mange:
L'homme, au Sacrement couvert,
Et l'ange, au Ciel, descouvert.[50]

His first affirmation is that fundamental notion of Christ's presence in this:

tressaint, sacré et tressouverain Sacrifice et Sacrement de la Messe,...mystere ineffable qui comprend l'abisme de la charité divine.[51]

This presence he confesses in faith as the Scripture has revealed it to him and as the Church has transmitted it to him by tradition. All during his life Francis will continue to affirm this primordial aspect of the Eucharist.

This position is different from the Calvinist notion of Théodore de Bèze in our preceding analysis of the "Confession." But before juxtaposing the two confessions, we should like to consider how Francis sees this presence taking place and then its significance.

E.   EUCHARIST IS THE PRESENCE OF THE RISEN CHRIST

Francis teaches that the Church has always believed in the real presence of Christ in the bread and wine. He cites on this subject the Council of Trent:

Le Concile de Trente, en la session treysiesme, chap. premier, parle ainsy:

---

50.   *Ibid.*, XXII, pp. 107-108.

51.   *Ibid.*, III, p. 100.

"Le saint concile enseigne et confesse ouvertement et simplement, qu'au tres auguste Sacrement de la sainte Eucharistie, apres la consecration du pain et du vin, Nostre Seigneur Jesus Christ, vray Dieu et vray homme, est contenu vrayement, reelement et substantiellement souz l'espece de ces choses sensibles."[52]

He will try to show that this conciliar affirmation must be distinguished from an imagined carnal presence and that this real presence is that of the risen Christ. The Calvinist doctrines have already stated that Catholics for them are:

antropophages ou mangegens, cannibales et margajas, qui s'entremangent les uns les autres.[53]

Francis will counteract this notion by, first, showing that the Body of Christ can be "reellement" and "spirituellement" present in the Eucharist. We find this Eucharistic doctrine in a series of sermons that he gave in 1597 in the Chablais. He will begin with the definition of the terms "reellement" and "spirituellement." Then he will consider the three modes of the presence of a body.

The presence of a body can initially be conceived of "naturellement et charnellement," as "mon cors est praesent a ceste chare, et les vostre a vos sieges," a real presence, "car c'est la propre essence et substance de nos cors qui y est," but a "charnelle" presence because

c'est avec toutes les qualités naturelles de nostre chair, la pesanteur, espaisseur, mortalité, obscurité, et semblables marques de nostre misere et propre nature.

Considered in this way the body is present "reelement" and "non spirituellement," because, he adds in the same text:

c'est la façon ordinaire et naturelle de la presence de nos cors et de tous les cors de ce bas monde, selon laquelle aussi peuvent ilz estre mangés.[54]

---

52. *Ibid.*, XXIII, pp. 244-245.

53. *Ibid.*, VII, p. 323.

54. *Ibid.*, p. 322.

52

The intelligence and the memory can give us the presence of a body in a second way; that is "spirituellement" and "not really." However, this is a metaphorical mode of presence of Jesus in the hearts of believers.[55]

Having thus specified these two modes of presence, Francis shows that the presence of Christ in the bread and wine, as His body and blood, proceeds from a third mode of presence. The body of Christ is simultaneously present but "reellement" and "spirituellement" and so one can really and spiritually consume "tout ensemble."

Francis asks himself first: "How did the bread become the body of Christ?" His response is simply:

> Il se peut faire par un changement total de substance en substance, que l'on appelle fort proprement du mot de transsubstantiation.[56]

What is his argument? Jesus is really present in the Eucharist, but without a quantitive, actual extension; that is, it is not bound to a quantity of dimension. A first aspect is "internal extension" which is the internal cohesion of the body in its juxtaposition of the parts which comprise it. The second effect, the "external extension" which is the relationship of the body with the exterior. The relationship of the parts is within space and time. Francis insists on this "intérier-extérieur" coupling.

The internal extension is essential to all bodies and normally is accompanied by the external extension. But metaphysically it is not proven that this second effect always accompanies the first and that it cannot be separated from it. We can conceive of a "mode surnatuel d'être" of a body whose external extension might be separated from the internal extension in such a way that the body exists without occupying space. For example, a concept or an original idea can bring about an industrial complex. Concretely this complex can exist integrally in its concept alone - without possessing an external extension which can only exist as a result of the creative will that brings it to a new form of existential reality. This concerns

55.   Ibid., p. 323.

56.   Ibid., p. 335.

then a presence that does not possesss a particular mode of quantity or dimension, but rather, to use scholastic terminology, the mode of substance.

Francis says that the real presence of Our Lord:

> est en l'Eucharistie sans y occuper place. Il y est les parties bien proportionnees ensemble, mays sans aucune proportion de place parce qu'elles n'en occupent point.[57]

He uses a Thomistic notion dealing with the presence of spirits. In effect, St. Thomas states that it is proper to the spirit to be omnipresent to and in each part because the spirit does not possess quantity nor does its substance depend on quantity. The body of Christ is not a spirit, but it depends on this category because it participates in the property of the spirit in relationship to the species under which it is contained. The body of Christ is in the Eucharist without abandoning its corporality, but insofar as its mode of existence is concerned, it participates in the prerogative of the spirit.

In another sermon, before 1597, we find a summary of this whole presentation:

> Pour les Catholiques, le Christ comme homme est réellement présent, non pas partout, mais dans son Sacrement, dans le Ciel et où il lui plait. Et d'abord, il est réellement présent dans l'Eucharistie, d'une manière spirituelle, Ainsi, il sortira demain du sépulcre, réellement, mais d'une manière invisible; comme l'Ange, au contraire, sera vêtu de blanc visiblement. Merveilleux échange! On verra un esprit, on ne pourra voir un corps. De même, lundi, vous verrez le Christ pèlerin, faire tout un voyage sans être connu. Le corps de Jésus-Christ est donc dans l'Eucharistie, et non seulement son corps, mais encore son sang, son âme vivante et vivifiante et sa divinité.[58]

So Francis brings out the fact that the body of Christ is really present in the Eucharist. If it is invisible, this is because visibility of a substance depends on its quantity and its proportions. All this argumentation depending on an original exegesis by Francis is difficult for us in the 20th century. However, this was sufficient for Francis to counteract the Protestant argument current in his time. Of course, Francis also used a great deal of sacred scripture in

---

57. *Ibid.*, p. 334.

58. *Ibid.*, p. 288 (original text is in Latin).

54

his argumentation, but to delve into this here would be too long for our present purpose.

In a way different from the Reformers, Francis de Sales envisages the Eucharist as a sign of God's love for man:

> Voudries vous bien,...qu'un morceau de pain, un legs si petit, fut le gage d'un tel et si grand amour? Non c'estoit luy mesme en une autre forme, impassible, qu'il donnoit comme un juste et asseuré testmoignage de l'exces de son amour.[59]

And Francis continues by developing a whole series of arguments based on law, tradition, the Fathers of the Church and several spiritual authors.

The words of consecration are for him of a limpid clarity. One could not question the words of institution of the Eucharist:

> cette parole du Christ, plus claire que le soleil, plus inébranlable que le firmament: 'Ceci est mon corps.'[60]

For Francis there can be no doubt. Because Jesus took bread and said: "This is my body," He is really present in the sacrament that He instituted:

> Nostre Seigneur prit du pain et dict: Cecy est mon cors. Donq ce n'est plus pain si c'est le cors de Nostre Seigneur; car si ce qu'il prit en ses benistes mains n'estoit pas changé, il ne falloit pas dire que ce fut autre chose que ce qui estoit auparavant. Auparavant c'estoit pain, maintenant c'est son cors; donques il est changé de pain en cors.[61]

Francis teaches that Jesus Christ is really present under the forms of bread and wine. One realizes this truth by means of one's faith. He/she admits a difference in the mode of apprehension of this presence and that of the presence of the sensible realities. This is because in the Eucharist there is a completely different presence; that is, a spiritual or immediate one. There is not the concept of distance that there is in our presence in the world. This immediate presence takes on its sense in the risen Christ in His glory. This presence is an exception to the notions of space and of time. It is

---

59.   *Ibid.*, p. 346.

60.   *Ibid.*, XXIII, p. 93 (original text is in Latin).

61.   *Ibid.*, VII, p. 336.

this risen Christ who alone can be identified with his body without a concept of distance being involved. In the plan of a sermon for the feast of the Ascension, Francis deals with this notion of immediacy:

> c'est un article de foi que Jésus 'est monté aux cieux, il n'est donc pas dans l'Eucharistie';...Toute la raison de l'acte est dans la toute - puissance de Celui qui agit.[62]

So Christ tells us:

> Ceci est mon corps; pourquoi hésites-tu? Assurément c'est le corps du Christ.[63]

And Francis continues:

> 'Elie laisse à son disciple son manteau;[64] le Fils de Dieu montant au Ciel, nous laisse sa chair; mais Elie s'était dépouillé, le Christ, lui, nous laisse sa chair sans la quitter lui-même,' bien qu'il la cache. Mais enfin il y a plus. Loin de contredire l'Eucharistie, l'Ascension lui sert d'appui. Voyez en effet, je vous prie, ce corps, non plus charnel, mais spirituel, qui pénètre les cieux.[65]

Therefore, the presence of the risen Christ is invisible but not less real.

This is difficult for us. We easily understand that our body really is "ours," but, at the same time, it is a "stranger" to us because we cannot actually be without it and yet we do not have complete domination over it. The body of the risen Christ seems to possess not only extraordinary qualities but even contradictory ones; it appears suddenly, it goes through walls, it can, or need not be, apprehended. And yet it remains a body that eats; one that can be touched. There is a presence that one feels. This is the way the first witnesses of the risen Christ apprehended and described this presence.[66]

After the Ascension, Christians have continued, and continue today, to encounter this human body of Jesus and to consume it in the Eucharist.

Without matter we cannot conceive of birth, knowledge or conscience. It is directly or indirectly through matter that we become intellectually

---

62. *Ibid.*, VIII, p. 23.

63. *Ibid.*, p. 24.

64. 4 Kings, 11, 13.

65. *Oeuvres*, VIII, p. 24 (original text is in Latin).

66. Luke XXIV, 13-35, John XX, 24-29.

awakened. It is through our mind that we are able to conceive of a spiritual existence, though completely independent of it. Because this matter is for us what essentially limits and defines, we exclude it totally from the idea of God. This implies that God has no body or that this body is not imaged as an organic unity or a unified, homogenous, stable whole.

Thus if God is present in the Eucharist in a bodily way that He Himself has chosen, there is a mode of presence proper to this body. But this presence necessarily implies a life-giving soul because this is necessary to the human being.

Francis de Sales teaches that Jesus Christ's life-giving soul is present in the Eucharist. The Incarnate Word exists as prototype of creation in the Eucharist.

It is in this language of the heart, of affectivity that St. Francis de Sales invites his followers to approach the Risen One in His real presence. This involves the very crux of Salesian thought; the love of God in Christ within the very heart of humanity itself.

Francis founds his theology on this God of love whom we can know through revelation. From his revelation by Jesus Christ, the Word of God Himself, we are able to attain the reality of the Risen One and His presence in the Eucharist. God is love; a love expressed in the Incarnation and creation. But as man refuses this love, God shows us the reality of it through the death of His Son on the cross. It is this death that the Spirit vivifies and gives to the Church. This spirit-life is the existence of the risen One!

Man is enabled to share in this spirit-life through the glorified body of Christ. With St. Paul,[67] Francis makes this profession of faith:

> L'homme es composé d'ame et de corps; et, bien que la mort, qui est entrée au monde par le peché, les separe, cependant nous esperons et croyons en la "resurrection de la chair," par laquelle nos miserables corps seront reunies à nos ames, et par cette reunion ils participeront à leur gloire et felicité, ou à leur peine et condamnation eternelle.[68]

---

67.   Philippians XIII, 20-21.

68.   *Oeuvres*, IX, p. 370.

This eternal glory will be manifested in the conversation with the glorified humanity of Christ:

> O si nous pouvions comprendre quelque chose de la consolation que les Bienheureux ont en parlant de cette amoureuse mort, combien nos ames se delecteroyent d'y penser![69]

But as men we must freely choose this conversation with Christ. The summit of our nature is our free will, our liberty:

> Quoy que le Saint Esprit, comme une source d'eau vive, aborde de toutes pars nostre coeur pour respandre sa grace en iceluy, toutefois, ne voulant pas qu'elle entre en nous sinon par le libre consentement de nostre volonté, il ne la versera point que selon la mesure de son bon playsir et de notre propre disposition et cooperation.[70]

The Word, through His incarnation, simultaneously took this human liberty and showed us that we too must bring about our salvation because as human beings we possess "l'inclination d'aymer Dieu sur toutes choses."[71] That is, this liberty and this inclination have been realized, supernaturalized in the person of the Son of God. So our nature is ordained to that supernature and redemption as its completion. It is through Christ that the work of creation is brought to its proper end.[72] Man is destined to seek to transform his nature into a super-nature. Thus there is between nature and super-nature the same difference that there is between him who wishes to love and him who can love; we can love only through Christ who has given us the power of becoming children of God in taking on our nature.

It is at this point where the Eucharist enters the Salesian tableau. If we are created to love in the image of God, that implies that we are conscious of it; conscious of being made for the purpose of love. And we know this by the Word of God, the Word made flesh in time in order to perfect and supernaturalize us. It is He who initiates each day for us a new

---

69. *Ibid.*, X, p. 243.

70. *Ibid.*, IV, pp. 121-122.

71. *Ibid.*, p. 77.

72. *Ibid.*, pp. 102-105.

Incarnation, in man himself through the Spirit. In the Eucharist is the creation which embodies all matter as well as man's production of the bread and the wine that are necessary prior to consecrating them:

> Nostre Seigneur est le premier, l'Alpha et l'Omega, c'est à dire le commencement et la fin de toutes choses...le Sauveur vint pour recreer l'homme, car il s'estoit perdu....C'est pourquoy Nostre Seigneur venant le renouveller, commença cette recreation comme il avoit fait la creation....Il a voulu donner entrée à l'Evangile par ce premier signe de la conversion et transmutation de l'eau en vin; il a aussi voulu donner fin à ses predications par la transformation du vin an sang. Il a fait le premier miracle en un banquet, il fit le dernier, celuy de l'Eucharistie, en un autre banquet. Il changea l'eau en vin aux noces de Cana en Galilée, et en ce dernier souper qui fut comme les noces de cet Espoux sacré, il convertit le pain en sa chair et le vin en son sang; de sorte qu'en cette transformation il commença à solemniser ces noces qu'il acheva sur l'arbre de la croix, car la mort du Seuveur fut le jour de ses noces.[73]

It is the Eucharist then which permits us to attain the reality of the risen Christ. It is with him alone, in the glory of his resurrection that all this is rendered possible; that love takes on its true sense. By the risen Christ, we can really aspire to eternity, the final resurrection which will be the reunion of our body and soul, in that life which is promised us. We shall be completely immersed in the love of God in the general act of transformation which seeks that, from the least particle of living matter to the purest of spirit, the whole universe be Christ's and participate in the glory of God.

It is at this point where Salesian christocentricism united to a profound knowledge of love takes on its full significance!

In order to understand the sacraments and the Eucharist in Salesian theology, we must always begin with this plan of the love of God. Francis expresses the reality and the efficacy of the Eucharistic union of love in a letter to St. Jeanne de Chantal. This letter is one of the most beautiful expressions of his affective language:

> Ceux qui font bonne digestion corporelle ressentent un renforcement par tout leur cors, par la distribution generale qui se fait de la viande en toutes leurs parties. Ainsy, ma Fille, ceux qui font bonne digestion spirituelle ressentent que Jesus Christ, qui est leur viande, s'espanche et communique a toutes

---

73.   *Ibid.*, X, pp. 4-5.

les parties de leur ame et de leur cors. Ilz ont Jesus Christ au cerveau, au coeur, en la poitrine, aux yeux, aux mains, en la langue, aux orielles, aux pieds. Mais, ce Sauveur, que fait il par tout par la? Il redresse tout, il purifie tout, il mortifie tout, il vivifie tout. Il ayme dans le coeur, il entend au cerveau, il anime dans la poitrine, il void aux yeux, il parle en la langue, et ainsy des autres: il fait tout en tout, et lhors nous vivons, non point nous mesmes, mais Jesus Christ vit en nous. O quand sera-ce, ma chere Fille? mon Dieu, quand sera-ce?[74]

This passage brings out the originality of the eucharistic presence. In expressing the biological assimilation of food by the body, Francis expresses the symbolism best fitted to signify this presence; our body can live only by the elements which it absorbs. It is only in this way that we can live in the divine life by the reception of the bread of life, the risen Jesus Christ. This fundamental symbolism is present to each civilization. It expresses simultaneously the immediate and intimate reality: "He lives in me and I in Him."[75]

Nulle union plus grande que la nourriture, 'Ils seront deux en une seule chair.'[76] C'est pourquoi la béatitude est comparée à un souper et à une manducation.[77]

This is the ordinary meaning given to the eucharistic meal and to Communion.

Having considered these several points, we should now like to deal with three aspects of the Eucharist that are present in St. Francis' teachings: i.e., Eucharist as meal, sacrifice and memorial.

F.   *EUCHARIST AS MEAL*

Le Sauveur a institué ce Sacrement très auguste de l'Eucharistie qui contient reellement sa chair et son sang, "affin que qui le mange vive eternellement."[78, 79]

---

74.   *Ibid.*, XIII, pp. 357-358.

75.   John VI, 57.

76.   Genesis II, 24.

77.   *Oeuvres*, VIII, p. 12.

78.   John VI, 53-58.

79.   *Oeuvres*, III, p. 116.

The Eucharist is real nourishment. It is the meal where we eat and partake of the body and the blood of Christ.

a.   Specificity of the Eucharistic meal:

Every meal implies the eating of food. The eucharistic meal supposes foods. In this meal the bread is changed into the body of Christ. It becomes our nourishment as Francis shows us from the Old Testament:

> La manne était préparée par les mains des Anges; le pain de la Cène, par les boulangers. La manne vint du ciel, ce pain-ci vient du four....Sans travail comme le corps du Christ. Elle avait toute douceur et toute saveur.[80]

The manna was a real nourishment and not a representation; and so it is in the case of the Eucharist. From these Old Testament figures Francis speaks to us of the reality of this nutrition: manna, paschal lamb, signifying the alliance between God and his people. This alliance is sealed, not by certain representations, but in the "manducation" of the nutrition received as manna or offered as the paschal lamb:

> Et saint Jan l'apelle (le Christ) Agnus Dei. Maintenant voyons son excellence avec celle du pain, si le pain seul y est. 1. Quant à la substance; c'est évident. 2. Quant à la signification: la chair est mieux représentée par de la chair que par du pain; la mort l'est mieux par la mort que par la fraction; l'innocence du Christ, par un agneau immaculé.[81]

This nourishment which gives life to our being maintains it in the same way as "corporal" nutrition gives life to our body. Our biological life is assured by the assimilation of food. So it is for our supernatural life which is guaranteed by the assimilation of this spiritual nourishment that we receive in the body and the blood of Christ.

> Le pain matériel entretient la vie, mays il y a bien a sçavoir comment; car comment, estant une chose morte, il peut donner la vie? L'homme l'altere peu a peu et le change en chair, alaquelle il donne la vie; et ainsy le pain continue la vie quil a receu, comme matiere mieux disposée.[82]

---

80.   *Ibid.*, VII, p. 272 (text in Latin).

81.   *Ibid.*

82.   *Ibid.*, p. 183.

Therefore, Christ is the veritable nourishment in the eucharistic meal. From this we can draw some conclusions regarding its signification.

  b.   Signification of the eucharistic meal:

Francis sees three "proprietés singulieres de ce pain celeste".[83]

  1)   The gift of the life of Christ Himself which leads to a perfect intimacy with Him.

> ce celeste pain ne reçoit la vie de celuy qui le mange, mays la luy donne absolument et le change en luy.[84]

  2)   This intimacy with Christ is primarily the transformation of our being into the being of Christ Himself:

> Ce pain, et voyci un seul motif, nous transforme en luy, non ja quand a la substance mais quand aux qualités.... 'Je vis non plus moi, mais le Christ vit en moi.'[85, 86]

  3)   Finally, this bread which intimately unites us to the Risen One strengthens us, fortifies us, 'nous corrobre interieurement.'[87]

However, this Christ life in us, that the eucharistic bread gives us, if it:

> nous corrobore interieurement, mais il ne nous rend formidable extérieurement; il (ce pain) nous praeserve dedans, mais dehors non.[88]

It is the recollection of our human condition that produces the awareness that total union with the risen One will be accomplished in the hereafter. For the moment, the Eucharist is only the promise of that eschatalogical time. During this moment, we are in a situation of becoming. We have the Christ life in us, but this life is to be acquired everyday in all that we do.

---

83.   *Ibid.*

84.   *Ibid.*

85.   Galatians, II, 20.

86.   *Oeuvres*, VII, p. 183.

87.   *Ibid.*, p. 184.

88.   *Ibid.*

The Eucharist then is a "gift" of Christ in faith, a gift which strengthens and assimilates us to Him. For the believer, this gift must correspond to an "intentionality" to receive it.

G. *EUCHARIST AS SACRIFICE*

It is scriptural sources that Francis draws on in order to teach us that the eucharistic meal is a sacrifice. The words of institution leave no room for doubt on this point:

> Par les paroles: datur, Luc 22; et effunditur pro vobis et pro multis.[89]

> Quoi de plus clair, en effect que ces paroles: Ceci est mon corps qui est donné pour vous; Ceci est mon sang qui est répandu pour vous et pour plusieurs en rémission des péchés?[90]

The sacrifice of Christ is the new alliance of God with us. This notion is rooted at the very heart of all the civilizations where sacrifice is at the center of all relationship with the divinity:

> car en toute loi il y a le sacrifice, même dans la loi de nature sous sa forme la plus simple.[91]

In God's plan for humanity, sacrifice has always held an important place as the seal of the alliance between God and the Jewish people. This is clear in Psalm 110. The offering of the high priest Melchisedech is manifestly a sacrifice. The prophet Malachi also offers a sacrifice.[92]

Considering sacrifice in this way, Francis tries to clarify its signification. He uses the Tridentine doctrine of the sacrifice of the Mass as his point of departure:

> il n'y a pas, en effet, deux sacrifices, celui de la Croix et celui de l'autel, mais un seul, parce que, d'un côté comme de l'autre, c'est une même chose qui est offerte, par un même sacrificateur, à une même fin et au même père....la différence n'est que dans la manière et la forme....sur la croix il est offert

---

89.   *Ibid.*, VII, p. 229.

90.   *Ibid.*, XXIII, p. 99.

91.   *Ibid.*, VII, p. 229 (text in Latin).

92.   Malachi, I, 11.

dans sa propre apparence et forme, d'une manière sanglante, tandis que dans l'Eucharistie, il l'est sous l'espèce du pain et du vin, selon l'ordre de Melchisédech, d'une manière non sanglante.[93]

It is then in the cross, in the Paschal mystery that the eucharistic sacrifice takes its signification.

The Eucharist is a veritable sacrifice, applying the sacrifice of the cross although it contains only a representation of the real immolation of the cross. Faithful to the Council of Trent,[94] Francis gives us the sense of the eucharistic sacrifice in this outstanding image:

Le soleil, par un acte unique et continu, offre et communique sa lumière au monde inférieur et n'est aucunement affecté en lui-même par l'alternance des nuits et des jours, bien que, par rapport à nous, la diversité des nuits et des jours nous fasse distinguer en lui un cours sans cesse recommencé dans son unité. Ainsi donc, celui qui dirait que le sacrifice de la Messe et celui de la Croix sont deux sacrifices, dirait vrai à cause de la forme et des modes divers de la double offrande; mais il est bien mieux et non moins vrai, tout au contraire plus vrai, de parler d'un seul sacrifice, à cause de l'identité, pour ainsi dire, de Celui qui à la fois offre et est offert, de Celui à qui il est offert et de la fin pour laquelle il est offert. C'est comme pour le soleil: celui qui parlera d'un seul, à cause de l'unité indivise de la substance du soleil, s'exprimera avec plus de vérité que celui qui, à cause de la distinction des jours, estimera devoir parler de plusieurs soleils.[95]

Meal and sacrifice, the Eucharist is the manifestation of God's love for the world expressed by the presence there of the risen Christ. This presence is an effective one because it is a continual memorial of the Last Supper.

H. *EUCHARIST AS MEMORIAL*

It seems evident to Francis de Sales that the Eucharist is the memorial of the Last Supper of the Lord. We have felt this in the reading of the many texts cited above. However, there is not a strong development of this point in his writings. In this respect, Francis follows the tradition of the Church. For the disciples of Christ, the Fathers and authors right up to the

93. *Oeuvres*, XXIII, p. 103.

94. Dumeige, G., *La foi catholique*, Orante, Paris, 1961, pp. 420-422.

95. *Oeuvres*, XXIII, p. 105.

64

16th Century, the memorial of the Last Supper of the Lord is so clear that there is no need to develop the point. But what is behind this assumption? What truly is the Eucharist considered as a memorial? Francis is very explicit in the Fabrien Code in restating the traditional affirmation. The eucharistic sacrifice:

> n'est pas tant la répétition de l'offrande faite sur la croix, que sa continuation et sa reproduction persévérante, puisque l'acte de volonté par lequel le Christ Rédempteur s'est offert et s'offre pour toujours au Père, est unique, perpétuel et très constant.[96]

The Eucharist is then, the actualization, the renewal in the Church of the Last Supper of the Lord. This is the response of the Church which is obedient to Christ's command: "Do this in memory of me."[97] The Bishop of Geneva does not, therefore, reduce the Eucharistic meal to a simple commemoration of the Last Supper. Furthermore, for him this would not be sensible. The Last Supper is not simply a chance occurrence. Rather, it is a sacrament, a significant act oriented towards another event. Its sense is derived from that other event which is no other than the death and the resurrection of Christ.

It is the mystery of the passion:

> car l'Eucharistie le represente principalement a rayson de la totale identité de celuy lequel y est offert et de Celuy qui fut offert sur la Croix, qui n'est qu'un mesme Jesus Christ.[98]

In actualizing the Last Supper of the Lord, it is not really the Last Supper that the Church presents to us but much more; it is that which is signified, that which is represented: the Lord's Pasch. There cannot be a true memorial, true actualization of the Last Supper unless it is reproduced for what it truly is, the sacrament of Christ's Pasch. In recalling the Last Supper, the Church actually performs again the thanksgiving of Christ, as He did, during the meal and with the same words that he employed.

---

96. *Ibid.*, p. 104.

97 Luke, XXII, 19:1 Corinthians II, 25.

98 *Oeuvres*, II, p. 216.

We shall conclude here our very brief study of the Eucharist in Salesian theology. It is perfectly clear that Francis de Sales teaches a very traditional and classical doctrine which is faithful to the tradition of the Church and most particularly to the Council of Trent. His place in the Counter Reformation is a very clear and decisive one.

It remains for us now to juxtapose the eucharistic doctrines of Théodore de Bèze and Francis de Sales. Placed in a historical and theological context, this parallel study will reveal the struggle waged by each of our protagonists. It distinctly clarifies those eucharistic doctrines which were to reign in the respective churches for ensuing centuries.

La Colloque tenu à Poissy le 9 Septembre, 1561.

Le Colloque tenu à Poifsy le 9. Septembre, 1561.

A. Le Roy.
B. La Reyne Mere.
C. Monfieur.
D. Madame.
E. Le Roy de Nauarre.
F. La Reyne de Nauarre.

G. Princes du fang afsis derriere le Roy.
H. Gentilhommes de la chambre du Roy.
I. Table de Labeffe.
K. Cardinal de Lorrayne.
L. Cardinal de Tournon.

M. Cardinal de Chafillon.
N. Le Chancelier.
O. Eufques & Docteurs.
P. Cardinal d'Armagnac.
Q. Cardinal de Bourbon.
R. Cardinal de Guife.

S. Theodore de Beze qui parle.
T. Miniftres eftans auec luy.
V. Table des Religieufes.
X. Gardes du corps du Roy.
Y. Suiffes gardes du Roy.
Z. Secretaires d'Eftat

A. Le Roy.

B. La Reyne Mere.

C. Monsieur.

D. Madame.

E. Le Roye de Navarre.

F. Le Reyne de Navarre.

G. Princes du sang assis derriere le Roy.

H. Gentilhomm es de la chambre du Roy.

I. Table de labesse.

K. Cardinal de Lorayne.

L. Cardinal de Tournon.

M. Cardinal de Chatillon.

N. Le Chancelier.

O. Evesques & Docteurs.

P. Cardinal d'Armagnac.

Q. Cardinal de Bourbon.

R. Cardinal de Guise.

S. Theodore de Beze qui parle.

T. Ministres avec luy.

V. Table des Religieuses.

X. Gardes du corps du Roy.

Y. Suisses gardes du Roy.

Z. Secretaires d'Etat.

CHAPTER III

Théodore de Béze & François de Sales

In our first two chapters, we have tried to expose some of the eucharistic doctrine of Théodore de Bèze and St. Francis de Sales. We see in the first instance, the type of Reform thinking that led to the convocation of the Council of Trent. Subsequently, the eucharistic teaching of Francis de Sales was a direct consequence of the decisions of the bishops and theologians of this same council. The first type of thought provoked the council. The second was what the Church resolved as its future sacramental and particularly eucharistic teachings for the next three centuries.

Before proceeding with the historical setting that brought the two church leaders to their three meetings, we should like to point out an aspect of the history and theology of the period in which we are working: i.e., the Renaissance.

A. *THE RENAISSANCE*

The Renaissance in Europe is dated roughly from the 14th to the 16th century. During this period there was a revival of letters and art in Europe. This rebirth marked the transition from medieval to modern history. This type of change favored a very powerful intellectual and spiritual fermentation. Our two authors are very much the product of this humanistic renaissance.

They are integral to an intellectual movement which is characterized by the decline of scholastic theology. Theologians of this period are more apt to criticize than to replace the great theological and philosophical syntheses of the 12th and 13th centuries. The Scotch Franciscan Duns Scotus (1270-1308) will tend to separate philosophical knowledge, based on reason, from theological knowledge based on revelation. William of Ockham (1290-1350) will bring his nominalist theory to the fore throughout the civilized world. In this new approach, the natural sciences will be favored and metaphysics will be relegated to an inferior level. Theology leaves the universe of reason and depends entirely on revelation and personal intuition. Conciliarist theories arise at this time that lead directly to placing in question the authority and the infallibility of the Church. Reform of the Church becomes the commonplace of the day.

The Renaissance itself brought into existence the period of humanism. This system or attitude is characterized by the rediscovery and study of the Greek and Roman classics and by an emphasis on cultural and practical interests rather than on religion or the world of nature. Both of the authors we are considering were exemplary humanists during their lives. Henri Bremond points this out extensively in his study of spiritual writers in France in the 17th century and most notably of Francis de Sales.[1] I have already designated this in other writings in the past.[2] But this humanistic trait is not less true in Théodore de Bèze. One has only to glance at the titles of his writings to realize his humanistic formation and characteristics.

But this renders the reading of their theology a bit more complicated from a certain point of view. Points of departure are at times vague. Reasoning processes are not always clear. Conclusions are not always the result of a clearly thought out rationale. Vocabulary and turn of phrase are often reminiscent of flowery Greek and Latin forms of writing or rhetorical expressions.

James Farge of Toronto's Pontifical Institute of Medieval Studies has brought this out in one of his writings:

---

1. Bremond, Henri. *Histoire littéraire du sentiment religieux en France depuis la fin des guerres de religion jusqu'à nos jours*. Paris: Bloud et Gay, 1929-1936. Vol. II

2. Marceau, William. *L'optimisme dans les oeuvres de Saint François de Sales*. Paris: Lethielleux, 1973, p. 122, 266, 274.

The hostility of many scholastic theologians and philosophers to the growing vogue of languages studies and rhetoric is aptly summed up by the theologian John Mair (Major): "Science has no need for pretty words"; and by Mair's disciple, Jan Dullaert: "The better the grammarian, the worse the theologian and dialectician."[3] Prior to the condemnation of Luther the (Paris) Faculty assemblies had largely ignored the academic squabbles between scholasticism and humanism. The leading Paris humanist, Lefèvre d'Etaples, had been summoned in 1515 to be "amicably interrogated" about his support of Johann Reuchlin and about the fact that his name as used in Rome by critics of the Faculty.[4]

Of course, Lefèvre d'Etaples was a close friend and collaborator of Théodore de Bèze. They were both equally humanistic.

In the introduction to this chapter, I simply want to bring out the fact that the comparison of the eucharistic doctrines of our two humanistic writers is different from the comparison, for example, of the doctrine of St. Thomas Aquinas and Alexander of Hales. The humanistic characteristics of the men themselves and eventually of their writings demands a particular mind set and adaptation according to the times and psychologies of the period of the Renaissance. This can be said eminently of him who seeks an understanding of two Christian humanists such as de Bèze and de Sales.

De Bèze's doctrine of the Eucharist is largely due to much of the scriptural exegesis that he did during the course of his whole life. In 1551 he published a translation of 34 psalms; in 1552 he added to the preceding the 40 psalms that Clement Marot had already translated. Finally, in December of 1561 he completed this psalter by the translation of the 67 remaining psalms.

In 1556 de Bèze published an annotated Latin translation of the Greek text of the New Testament under the title of *Novum Testamentum Domini nostri Jesu Christi latine jam olim e veteri interprete nunc denuo a Theodoro Beza versum cum ejusdem annotationibus in quibus ratio interpretationis redditur.*

---

3.   Elie, H. *Le traité de l'infini de Jean Mair.* Paris, 1938. p. 120.

4.   Farge, James. *Orthodoxy and Reform in Early Reformation France: The Faculty of Theology of Paris, 1500-1543.* Leiden: Brill, 1985. p. 170.

As Calvin debated at length with the Lutherans, so also did de Bèze. At Geneva in 1559 he published his *Controverse avec les luthériens Westphal et Hesshus sur la cène*. De Bèze opposes the Lutheran doctrine of Westphal with the Calvinist doctrine in his *De coena Domini plena et perspicua tractatio in qua J. Westphali calumniae postremum editae refelluntur*. He replies to Hesshus in 1561 in his Κρεωφαγία *sive cyclops* and in his Ονος συλλογιζόμενος *sive sophista, Dialogi duo de vera communicatione corporis et sanguinis Domini adversus Hesshusii somnia; his accessit abstersio aliarum calumniarum quibus aspersus est Joannes Calvinus ab eodem Hesshusio; perspicua explicatio controversiae de coena Domini per Theodorum Bezam*. He later continued this controversy with the Lutherans on the question of the Eucharist. In 1578 de Bèze published *Ad repetitas Jacobi Andreae et Nicolai Selnecceri calumnias responsio*. This was followed in the same year by *De corporis Christi omnipraesentia*.

I shall not list the many titles of his literary and historical works here. Suffice it to say that his poetry, tragedy and *Histoire des Eglises réformées au royaume de France depuis l'an 1521 jusqu'en 1563* have served many scholars and researchers over the course of the centuries. More than 90 works of varying subjects and lengths demonstrate his humanistic position of importance in the French literature and theology of the 16th century in Europe.

B. *THEODORE DE BÈZE & THE COLLOQUY OF POISSY*

In order to bring out the historical importance of de Bèze in the evolution of the Reformed doctrine of the Eucharist, we should like to cast him in his role of Reformation protagonist. This role he played in France at the colloquy of Poissy which took place in September and October of 1561. Catherine of Medici had invited Calvin himself to represent the Reformers in what she conceived as an ecumenical meeting. But the aging Calvin declined the invitation and asked his faithful friend to attend in his stead. De Bèze accepted and journeyed north of Paris to appear before the king, queen and high Roman churchmen of the kingdom of France. He was the leader of the Reformed delegation.

The child-king Charles IX opened the colloquy with a brief statement of intent:

> Messieurs, je vous ay fait assembler de divers lieux de mon royaume pour me donner conseil sur ce que vous proposera mon Chancelier, vous priant de mettre toute passion bas, afin nous en puissions receuillier quelque fruict qui tourne au repos de tous mes sujets, à l'honneur de Dieu, de l'acquit des consciences, et du repos public; ce que je desire tant, disoit il, que j'ay deliberé que vous ne bougiés de ce lieu, jusqu'à ce que vous y ayés donné bon ordre, que mes sujets puissent desormais vivre en paix et union les uns avec les autres, comme j'espere que vous ferés. Et ce faisant me donnerés occasion de vous avoir en la mesme protection qu'ont eu les Roys mes predecesseurs.[5]

Olivier Fatio states that the aims of the Protestants at Poissy were not the same as those of the queen-mother and many of the Catholic prelates:

> Peu interessés par les compromis iréniques vers lesquels plus d'un prélat catholique penchait, les réformés voyaient dans le colloque la possibilité, si longtemps attendue, d'expliquer et de justifier publiquement leur doctrine. Telle était leur confiance dans la vérité de cette doctrine qu'il suffisait à leurs yeux qu'elle fût exposée pour convaincre et triompher sans qu'il fût besoin de formules de concorde.[6]

It was Théodore de Bèze who would declare before this august assembly the Protestant doctrine. In his famous Harangue, pronounced on September 9, 1561 at the opening of the session, de Bèze presented this doctrine and included the main points of divergence: good works, the authority of Scripture, the Fathers and the Councils of the Church, the sacraments and finally ecclesiastical discipline. It is his treatment of the sacraments and of the Eucharist in particular that interests us here.

Baum et Cunitz record in detail the words of de Bèze in their *Histoire ecclésiastique des églises réformées au royaume de France*. In the French of the 16th century they record:

---

5. Baum, G. et Cunitz, E. *Histoire ecclesiastique des églises réformées au royaume de France*. Paris: Fischbacher, 1883, I, p. 556.

6. Fatio, Olivier, p. 11.

> Nous sommes d'accord, à nostre advis, en la description de ce mot Sacremens, c'est à savoir que les sacremens sont signes visibles, moyennant lesquels la conjonction que nous avons avec nostre Seigneur Jesus Christ, ne nous est pas simplement signifiée ou figurée, mais aussi nous est veritablement offerte du costé du Seigneur, et consequemment ratifiée, feellée, et comme engravée par la vertu du sainct Esprit en ceux qui par une vraye foy apprehendent ce qui leur est ainsi signifié et presenté. J'use de ce mot, signifié messieurs, non pour enerver ou aneantir les sacremens, mais pour distinguer le signe d'avec la chose qu'il signifie en toute vertue et efficace.[7]

As an experienced preacher and apologist, de Bèze presented adroitly the points of doctrine on which the two parties were in agreement. However, he courageously delivered the doctrine to which he ascribed:

> Nous accordons par consequent, qu'ès Sacremens il faut necessairement qu'il entrevienne une mutation celeste et supernaturelle. Car nous ne disons pas que l'eau du sainct Baptesme soit simplement eaue, mais qu'elle est un vray sacrement de nostre regeneration, et du lavement de nos ames au sang de Jesus Christ. Pareillement nous ne disons pas qu'en la saincte Cene de nostre Seigneur, le pain soit simplement pain, mais sacrement du precieux corps de nostre Seigneur Jesus Christ qui a esté livré pour nous.[8]

It is at this point where de Bèze denies the Catholic notion of the sacrament. He continues in applying the Reformed theology to the Eucharist:

> Et ne disons point aussi qu'elle se face par la vertu de certaines paroles prononcées, ni par l'intention de celuy qui les prononce, mais par la seule puissance et volonté de celuy qui a ordonné toute ceste action tant divine et celeste, duquel aussi l'ordonnance doit estre recitée haut et clair en langage entendu, et clairement exposée, afin qu'elle soit entendue et receue par ceux qui y assistent.[9]

De Bèze continues to seek those terms which will conciliate the two groups according to the wishes of the king and queen, but he is finally obliged to state his position clearly:

---

7.   Baum, G. et Cunitz, E. I. p. 572.

8.   *Ibid.*

9.   *Ibid.*

....Mais il nous semble, selon la petite mesure de cognoissance que nous avons receue de Dieu, que ceste transubstantiation ne se rapporte à l'analogie et convenance de nostre foy, d'autant qu'elle est directement contraire à la nature des sacremens, esquels il faut necessairement que les signes substantiels demeurent, pour estre vrais signes de la substance du corps et du sang de Jesus Christ, et est pareillement renversée la vérité de la nature humaine et ascension d'iceluy. Je dy le semblable de la seconde opinion qui est de la Consubstantiation, laquelle outre tout cela n'ha nul fondement sur les paroles de Jesus Christ, et n'est aucunement necessaire à ce que nous soyons participans du fruict des sacremens.[10]

The succeeding section of the oration of de Bèze is purported by some historians to have brought the doctors of the Sorbonne, the "periti" and other Catholic participants at the colloquy angrily to their feet:

Si quelcun là dessus nous demande si nous rendons Jesus Christ absent de la saincte Cene, nous respondons que non. Mais si nous regardons à la distance des lieux (comme il le faut faire, quand il est question de sa presence corporelle, et de son humanité distinctement considerée):[11] Nous disons que son corps est esloigné de pain et du vin, autant que le plus haut ciel est esloigné de la terre, attendu que quant à nous, nous sommes en la terre et les sacremens aussi; et quant à luy, sa chair est au ciel tellement glorifée, que la gloire, comme dit sainct Augustin, ne luy a point osté la nature d'un vray corps, mais l'infirmité d'iceluy....[12]

Having pronounced this doctrine of the Reformers, the documents that recount the event continue:

Ceste harangue fut prononcée d'une façon fort agreable à toute l'assistance, comme depuis ont confessé les plus difficiles et fascheus, et fut ouie avec une singuliere attention, jusqu'à ce que de Bèze sur la fin, parlant de la presence de Jesus Christ en la Cene, dit, que le corps de Jesus Christ, combien qu'il nous fust veritablement offert et communiqué en icelle, estait toutesfois aussi loin du pain que le haut des cieux est esloigné de la terre. Ceste seule parole (combien qu'il eust bien dit d'autres aussi contraires et repugnantes à la doctrine de l'eglise Romaine) fut cause que les prelats commencerent à bruire et murmurer dont les uns disoient: *Blasphemavit*: les autres se levoient pour s'en aller, ne pouvans faire pis à cause de la

---

10.   *Ibid.*, p. 573.

11.   *Ibid.*, p. 574.

12.   *Ibid.*

presence du Roy. Entre autres le Cardinal de Tournon, doyen des Cardinaux, qui estoit assis au premier lieu, requist au Roy et à la Royne, qu'on imposast silence à de Bèze, ou qu'il luy fust permis et à sa compagnie de se retirer.[13]

One can imagine the consternation. Not an irenic syllable from the mouth of de Bèze. Though he did try to calm the troubled prelates, the Cardinal of Tournon rose and addressed the King:

...de ne croire rien de ce qui avoit esté dit, mais qu'il voulust demeurer en la religion de ses ancestres depuis le Roy Clovis, en laquelle il avoit esté nourri et feroit entretenu par la Royne sa mere, dont il prioit la glorieuse vierge Marie et tous les benoits Saincts luy faire la grace.[14]

History has shown that the Catholics at Poissy did not react in the tolerant manner desired by the Queen Regent. We are interested here in the fact that this very important address, wherein every sentence is of weight, had a somewhat direct bearing on the subsequent course of the French Reformation. This is the more general consideration. The more special and personal has reference to Théodore de Bèze himself. As a work of art, the address at the Colloquy of Poissy exhibits, better, perhaps, than any of the other numerous works, the striking ability of the man whose name was instantly made famous. At the same time, its importance as an exposition of the theological views of de Bèze, and we may add, of Calvin, is paramount. The doctrinal contrast between the Reformation and the Roman Catholic system, on the one hand, and between the Reformers of Wittenberg and Zurich, on the other, is so clearly marked in this document that the most superficial of readers can have little difficulty in forming a distinct conception of the individuality of de Bèze as a theologian.

That his effort had proved a great success cannot be denied. Friends and foes were agreed on this point at least. Hubert Languet, the distinguished Protestant negotiator, who chanced to be in Paris at the time, expressed himself scarcely more strongly respecting the brilliancy of the oration than did Claude Haton, the curate of Provins. But whereas the Protestants gave it their unqualified approval, the Roman Catholics

---

13.   *Ibid.*, p. 578.

14.   *Ibid.*, p. 579.

condemned with great bitterness those utterances respecting the sacraments which had raised the passionate protests of Cardinal Tournon and his associates. There is no doubt that Catherine de Medici and others who shared her political views regarded de Bèze's frank statement as a needless and offensive expression of opinion, and deplored what they stigmatized as a blunder that came near wrecking the conference. But whoever will calmly consider the entire situation must come to a different conclusion. A suppression of the candid views of the Reformers on so critical a point might indeed have prevented an explosion of priestly indignation at this particular juncture. It could only have postponed what must have come sooner or later. Such difficulties are for the most part best met when met most promptly. A conference terminated because of a clear and unmistakable expression of opinion on an important theological subject - had indeed such a result ensued - would have wrought far less damage to the Protestant cause than might have resulted from an insincere and dishonest treatment of a distinctive dogma. The whole tone of the discussion could have been lowered by political silence and the self-respect of its professors would have been sacrificed. Calvin saw this, and far from condemning, he applauded de Bèze's boldness in unqualified terms:

> Oratio tua apud nos est, in qua Deus mirifice mentem et linguam tuam gubernavit. Quod bilem commovit sanctis patribus omnino testatum oportuit, nisi turpiter velles tergiversari, ac te objicere eorum probris, quos miror ea tantum de causa tumultuatos esse cum aliis locis non minus graviter vulnerati essent.[15]

De Bèze had nothing to retract and no apology to make. Hearing, however, that the queen-mother was, or pretended to be, displeased with what he had said on the matter of the Lord's Supper, he wrote to her, the next day, to explain both what he had said, which, because of the uproar created by the prelates, she had possibly not heard distinctly, and the object for which he had said it. Far from modifying his speech in any way, he repeated for Catherine's benefit the very words that had given offence. He

---

15.   Dufour, A. et Nicollier, B. *Correspondance de Théodore de Bèze*: recueillie par Hippolyte Aubert, Société du Musée Historique de la Réformation. Genève: Librairie Droz, 1960. III, p. 159 (24 septembre 1569).

declared that what had moved him to use them was a desire to defend his co-religionists from the charge of sacrilegiously absenting Jesus Christ from His Holy Supper. He wrote:

> Mais il y a grande difference de dire, que Jesus Christ est present en la saincte Cene, entant qu'il nous y donne veritablement son corps et son sang, et de dire que son corps et son sang font conjoincts avec le pain et le vin. J'ay confessé le premier, qui est aussi le principal; j'ay nié le dernier.[16]

De Bèze begged that he might be permitted to set forth his views more fully before her and any other persons who might give him instruction in case he were wrong. No such opportunity was granted him. The prelates, averse from the beginning to anything like free discussion with the Protestants, were still more disinclined to treat with them since they had heard the exposition of the Reformed doctrines by one who was at the same time forcible and gentle, courteous and self-possessed. But a promise had been given that de Bèze should be answered, and that promise the Cardinal of Lorraine undertook to redeem just one week after de Bèze had spoken. The place was the same; the assembled dignitaries were the same; the Protestants were the same except that their numbers were increased by the arrival of the distinguished Peter Martyr. And how did the cousin of the king reply to the clear and candid exposition of the Reformed faith made by de Bèze? Chiefly by an assumption of a lordly superiority, with a slight admixture of patronizing condescension and unsolicited compassion. On only two points of the Reformed confession did the cardinal even pretend to enter into argument. He maintained that the Church is no mere aggregation of the elect, but includes the weeds along with the wheat. He argued that the presence of the Lord in the Eucharist is not spiritual alone, but real and corporeal as well. As for the rest, he treated the Protestants as wayward but misguided children for whom he had no reproaches to utter, but only pity; they had shown some disposition to receive instruction and to return to a Church that was ready to welcome them as soon as they consented to submit to her authority.

---

16. Baum, G. p. 581.

On September 28, in a further effort to reconcile the two positions, the queen succeeded in convoking at Saint-Germain a group of five Catholic theologians and five Reformed theologians. Of course, the conclusions from these ten discussants were to be submitted to the official group still in session at Poissy. Théodore de Bèze was leader of the five at Saint-Germain.

Two documents on the Eucharist were successively sent from Saint-Germain to Poissy and rejected by the assembly. Finally, on October 3 the assembly decided to recall solemnly the Catholic confession of faith and to definitively censure the confession of the ministers.

Under the presidency of the Cardinal of Tournon on October 9, the prelates approved this censure and repeated the formulation of their faith. Following this, the Cardinal of Lorraine, terminating his role, pronounced the condemnation of anyone who held beliefs contrary. He insisted that the Reformers no longer be heard. The assembly voted for this motion. The colloquy of Poissy ended in failure.

Lucien Romier describes the conclusion of Poissy in the following manner:

> Sur la réforme des abus, l'assemblée laissait une série de décrets, que les cardinaux remirent à la Reine. Ces décrets, touchant uniquement la discipline ecclésiastique, visaient d'abord les clercs, évêques, officiers diocésains, chanoines, curés, simples prêtres, abbés commendataires, prieurs conventuels, moines et religieuses; un règlement corrigeait la liturgie, les offices et les pratiques cléricales; enfin un dernier texte tendait à modérer l'abus des censures et excommunications.[17]

Francis de Sales, in his relation with Théodore de Bèze, would not be impervious to the social conditions and ecclesiastical attitudes that we have seen permeate what Queen Catherine had hoped would be much more peaceful and irenic in France at this early point in the French Reformation.

In fact, Francis de Sales will live in a French climate of the turn of the century. It will have been conditioned by the refusal of some Catholic churchmen to seek a dialogue that might lead them along an ecumenical

---

17.   Romier, Lucien. *Catholiques et Huguenots à la Cour de Charles IX*. Paris: Perrin, 1924. p. 236.

road. Alain Dufour summarizes what happened as a result of the meeting at Saint-Germain:

> Emportée par un esprit de réaction, l'Assemblée procéda ensuite à une condamnation en règle, article par article, de toute la confession de foi des Eglises réformés de France, celle que l'on connaît sous le nom de Confession de La Rochelle. Ainsi se termina le Colloque de Poissy. Il y eut, au début de 1562, quelque tentative de remettre un project semblable sur pied, avec les conférences de Saint-Germain, mais ce fut une tentative beaucoup plus modeste et qui n'eut pas de succès non plus. Aussitôt commencèrent les guerres civiles; plus tard, il ne fut plus possible même d'y songer, car le Concile de Trente, achevé, faisait sentir ses effets; la doctrine catholique était désormais enfermée dans des définitions beaucoup plus strictes et intouchables que par le passé.[18]

C. *FRANÇOIS DE SALES & THE COUNCIL OF TRENT*

The Council of Trent would influence the young Francis de Sales who was born in 1567. The three sessions of the Council of Trent are dated by historians as having taken place between 1545 and 1563. Therefore, the very climate of the Counter-Reform determined by the decrees of the Council of Trent, was that in which the young Francis would be born, reared, educated and finally exercise his apostolate.

Both his mother and father were exemplary Roman Catholics. His primary education in Savoy was within religious institutions. He chose to be formed at the secondary level by the Jesuits at the College of Clermont in Paris rather than to go to the College of Navarre where the young noblemen of the French provinces normally were enrolled. Important to note here is that the Jesuits were founded with the very particular apostolate of the implementation of the Church's program of Counter-Reformation. The Jesuit Fr. Possevin was Francis' spiritual director during his doctoral studies in civil and canon law at Padua. Finally, in his jury at his doctoral defense were many of the most noted for their fidelity to the prescriptions of the Council of Trent. The former Jesuit provincial of the Paris province, Fr. André Ravier, writes in his most recent publication on St. Francis:

---

18.   Dufour, Alain. *Le colloque de Poissy*: *Mélanges d'histoire du XVIe siècle offerts à Henry Meylan.* Genève, 1970, pp. 135-136.

On Monday, March 22, 1599, Francis presented himself at the pontifical palace. The hall was filled with distinguished 'personages.' Eight cardinals were seated around His Holiness, among them Cardinal de Medici, Cardinal Borghesi, Cardinal Baronius, and Cardinal Borromeo; twenty archbishops and bishops; generals of religious orders. Father Bellarmine was prominent among the theologians responsible for debating with the candidate. This was indeed an honorary jury![19]

To have satisfied Pope Clement VIII and his particular group of theologians would have demanded profound penetration into, and complete conviction about the teachings of the Council of Trent. The thirty-five questions posed by such men as St. Charles Borromeo (1538-1584), nephew of Pope Pius IV, and the Jesuit theologian St. Robert Bellamine (1542-1621) could only manifest the absolute and unretractable fidelity of Francis de Sales to the teachings of the Council of Trent. They were to fashion the very principles of his personal and ecclesiastical existence.

After his doctoral studies, Francis chooses to become a priest. He becomes the provost of Bishop Granier. The latter is bishop of Geneva but now resident at Annecy due to the Huguenot presence in Geneva. Francis' installation as the provost of Geneva is described by Fr. Ravier:

On this occasion Francis delivered one of his most important speeches, a veritable 'keynote address,' by which all his activity as provost, then as prelate, would be inspired. The theme? 'We must regain Geneva.' The tone? It is a call to arms - to spiritual arms, to be sure! - the proof of which is that he dared call the 'venerable canons' his 'valiant comrades in arms.'[20]

Subsequently, Bishop Granier would name Francis to the missionary apostolate in a region of Savoy called the Chablais. This area between Geneva and Annecy had been won in great measure to Calvin's thought and practices. Francis would work here to regain these Huguenots to the Catholic Church.

Fr. Ravier describes this period:

In 1594 Charles-Emmanuel, the Duke of Savoy, had just won back the Chablais, which before the vicissitudes of the Reform constituted a part of his domain, but under the jurisdiction of

---

19.   Ravier, André. *Francis de Sales - Sage and Saint.* San Francisco: Ignatius Press, 1988. p. 99.

20.   *Ibid.*, p. 62.

the prince-bishop of Geneva. The religious situation had deteriorated gravely since the arrival of Calvinism in Geneva. Of the some twenty-five thousand souls who inhabited the area, only about a hundred Catholics remained.[21]

By the end of 1595, Francis' activity appears to have been prodigious. He preached, he catechized, he visited the sick, and if they were Catholic he brought them the Eucharist. A great part of his time was spent in talks with some Calvinists who came for discussions with him. He began to draw up the juridical code, which Antoine Favre had prepared (the celebrated *Code Fabrianus*) - as explanation of the principal heresies against which the legislator would have to guard: ardent pages that are among the most vigorous written by Francis; they would be included in a book Antoine Favre had prepared under the first title *De Summa Trinitate et Fide Catholica*. The better to confound the "heretics," Francis plunged into the study of the *Institutes of the Christian Religion* by Calvin, but not without having sought permission from Rome, humbly, like a simple cleric. All this in perspective, lest any jurist of the time think of calling him in question: "One faith, one law, one King." It was only little by little that Francis would arrive at harmonizing in himself the jurist and the apostle of Jesus Christ.

Dr. Ruth Kleinman prepared an enlightening thesis in Political Science at Columbia University: *Saint Francis de Sales and the Protestants*. She states in this thesis, later published in Geneva:

> ...the *Codex Fabrianus* represents the key to François de Sales' own attitude towards Protestant minorities in Catholic states. François de Sales began by accusing Calvin of having taught that the best form of government is a republic, whether controlled by a small group or by the people as a whole, and that, by inference, monarchy is the worst type of state. Monarchy might be tolerated, to avoid civil disorders, but not loved for its own sake. And this François de Sales exclaimed, from the subject of so great a prince. François de Sales, proceeding in the belief that Calvin was a republican, defended monarchy: the desirability of monarchy was proved not only by political theorists, but by Scripture, and even by nature.[22]

---

21. *Oeuvres*, XXIII, pp. 224-225.

22. Kleinman, Ruth. *Saint Francis de Sales and the Protestants*. Genève: Droz, 1962. p. 134.

Francis de Sales was a Catholic of his time. In his eucharistic convictions and teachings, he was a zealot of the Council of Trent. His civilization and Church formed him for what would be an encounter with the Calvinistic doctrines so adamantly adhered to in the second generation by Théodore de Bèze.

To return to the work of Kleinman, we see what I might call an "objective" interpretation of that which was the work of Francis de Sales in his early encounters with Reformed notions:

> What damages François de Sales' case irreparably in modern eyes is that he took out of context and misinterpreted every proposition he attributed to Luther and Calvin....Had François de Sales studied his authors objectively he could not have misunderstood them. What are we then to think of his arguments? At first glance, they show either a deliberate distortion of his opponents' statements, or at least ignorance on François de Sales' part. But he had taken pains with his research. As he wrote to Senator Favre, his contribution to the *Codex Fabrianus* cost him "infinite labor."[23] The question, therefore, is not whether François de Sales actually read the reformers, but how he read them....François de Sales was not analyzing the Protestant theory, whether political nor religious, for its merits. He started out by assuming it was wrong. Besides, according to his own experience, Protestant minorities in Catholic states were a politically unstable element....However questionable this method might seem to modern scholars, it was not uncommon in François de Sales' time....According to Francis de Sales, whoever attacked the Catholic Church destroyed the foundations of society....[24]

The Reformers were attacking the Church and the state in their new way of thinking. Reformation thought injured both the Church and the state. Therefore, fervent Catholic and monarchist, we must understand the behavior of this 16th-century priest, bishop and citizen.

D. *HISTORICAL NARRATIONS & THE ENCOUNTERS*

Francis de Sales and Théodore de Bèze had three meetings: each of them in Geneva. Most unfortunate is the fact that none of the documents

23. *Oeuvres*, XIII, p. 139.

24. Kleinman, R. p. 139.

from these encounters is in existence today. However, by the correspondence that does exist we are able to know of their having occurred.

The first meeting took place in Geneva on April 3, 1597. The young priest was 30 years of age. The venerable moderator of the Company of Pastors of Geneva was then 78. We learn of this occasion from a letter of Francis' to the then Pope Clement VIII.[25] In his letter of April 21, 1597 he writes of encountering de Bèze: "...lapideum deprehendi cor ejus, immotus hactenus, aut sane non omninoprobe commotum, inveteratum scilicet dierum malorum."[26]

The same Supreme Pontiff sent Francis a second brief on May 29.[27] He received this in Annecy on June 23. This provoked the second meeting of the two church leaders. Accompanied by his friend Senator Antoine Favre and his secretary Serge Sarget and George Rolland, he knocked at the door of Théodore de Bèze for the second time on July 3, 1597. This meeting's result did not fulfill the hopes of the young missionary any more than the first.

The third encounter took place sometime later. The Swiss historian, Paul F. Geisendorf, records the event with a rather salient commentary:

> Enfin dans une troisième visite, dont la date n'est point donnée, Sales aurait offert à Bèze de la part du pape une pension annuelle de quatre mille livres d'or, s'il se convertissait. Bèze aurait baissé les yeux, se serait tu pendant longtemps, puis aurait réitéré sa réponse à la Jeanne d'Arc. Les choses en seraient restées là, mais craignant de voir désormais Bèze céder à une nouvelle attaque, son entourage l'aurait surveillé plus étroitement, aurait empêché Sales de le revoir et étouffé ses plaintes comme ses velléités de repentir.[28]

His next paragraph expresses a major problem in much of the 16th-century's historical narration:

> Tous ces derniers traits sont parfaitement invraisemblables et l'on regrette de n'avoir pas été présent au procès de

---

25. *Oeuvres*, IX, pp. 268-270.

26. *Ibid.*, p. 270.

27. *Ibid.*, pp. 453-454.

28. Geisendorf, Paul-F. *Théodore de Bèze*. Genève: Jullien, 1967. p. 405.

canonisation pour demander aux témoins qui affirmaient ces choses comment donc ils les savaient, puisque aucun d'eux désormais n'avait eu le moyen d'approcher Bèze! Pour le reste du récit, et compte tenu des réserves qu'on vient d'esquisser, il est bien évident que, faute d'autres sources, on est réduit à le croire sur parole. Mais le réserve dont l'historien sérieux ne peut ni ne doit se départir en face d'une information si unilatérale, biographes et panégyristes de tout plume et de tout poil qui vont se succéder dans le temps n'en ont cure![29]

Reading the texts of Marsollier,[30] Lajeunie,[31] Ravier and others reveals a definite Catholic favoring position. On the other hand, the historical writings of Franck Puaux,[32] Dominic Fatio or Paul F. Geisendorf exemplify the Reform position. This particular difficulty has been treated by a very popular French Protestant sociologist and author Jean Baubérot.[33] He writes the following:

...une tradition historiographique, idéologiquement marquée par un climat oecuménique et progressivement hégémonique de par le développement de ce climat, tend à réduire les différences entre catholiques et protestants du XVIe et du XVIIe siècles, en réaction contre une historiographie antérieure. Le changement de termes de "Contre Réforme" à "Réforme catholique" est un aspect type de cette nouvelle tradition.[34] Certes la distance prise par rapport à un climat d'antagonisme confessionnel où existait le souci de conforter son camp a permis de percevoir certains parallélismes dans l'action des Églises de cette époque. Mais une idéologie de dialogue et de rapprochement comporte des aspects aveuglants, sur un plan heuristique, tout comme une idéologie

29. *Ibid.*, pp. 405-406.

30. Marsollier, M. *La vie de Saint François de Sales: évêque et prince de Genève et instituteur de l'ordre de la Visitation de Sainte Marie.* Paris, 1757.

31. Lajeunie, Etienne - Marie. *Saint François de Sales. L'homme, la pensée, l'action.* Paris: Victor, 1966.

32. Puaux, Franck. "Théodore de Bèze et Saint François de Sales," *Revue Chrétienne,* Paris, 1894. pp. 168-176.

33. Baubérot, Jean. "Le tricentenaire de la révocation de l'edit de Nantes," *Archives de sciences sociales des religions,* Oct-Dec. 1986, p. 192.

34. Venard, N. *Réforme, Réformation, Préréforme. Contre réforme...Etude de vocabulaire chez les historiens récents de langue française. Historiographie de la Réforme,* Paris, Delachaux et Niestlé, 1977.

84

de combat. Et de 'pieux silences' risquent d'aboutir à ce qu'Etienne Fouilloux appelle une 'autocensure oecuménique.'[35]

The reading of both Théodore de Bèze and Francis de Sales certainly shows a belligerent stance in both camps. The attitude of both the Protestant and Catholic representatives at the Colloque de Poissy reflects quite faithfully what were mutually antagonistic and opposed positions. There is certainly no suggestion of any ecumenical tendency in either church. It is much too early for this type of thinking. The initial notions of reform within the Church that were those of Luther and Calvin became polarized before long.

N. S. Davidson points to this in the introduction to his small book when he writes: "Luther a déclenché la Réforme parce qu'il croyait que Rome avait abandonné la vérité de l'Evangile. Ses contemporains ont développé le mouvement par leur allérgie à la corruption de l'Eglise."[36]

Each of our writers, de Bèze and Francis de Sales, was a product of his times and civilization. Their positions regarding the Church, politics, sacraments, etc. are a reflection of each of them in his own particular setting.

E. *POSITIONS OF THÉODORE DE BÈZE & FRANÇOIS DE SALES*

We are interested particularly in their concept of sacrament and of Eucharist. Having already presented their general positions in this area, de Bèze in the first chapter as a faithful follower of Calvin and Francis de Sales in Chapter II who reacts to the teaching of Luther and Calvin in being faithful to the doctrines of the Council of Trent, we now consider their positions regarding the following:

1. Sacrament
2. Transubstantiation
3. Mass as sacrifice

1. Sacrament:

Speaking against late scholastic theology, Luther and Calvin took as their point of departure the fact that Scripture is the primary source and sole

---

35. Fouilloux, E. "L'oecuménisme d'avant-hier à aujourd'hui," *Les Quatre Fleuves*, no. 20, 1984, p. 18.

36. Davidson, N. S. *La contre-réforme*. Paris: Cerf, 1989, p. 9.

ultimate norm for true theology. They both upheld that baptism and the Lord's Supper are enjoined upon the church by Jesus Christ and the church is not the church without them. Calvin held that baptism and the Lord's Supper must be administered by a properly ordained person. Théodore de Bèze was a model exemplar of this Reformer current of thought.

The thought of the Reformers was examined and categorically rejected by the Council of Trent. It considered the subject of the general doctrine on the sacraments in the seventh session. An explanation of the conciliar doctrine is found in thirteen canons. Its content clearly depends on the theology of St. Thomas Aquinas.

The Fathers of Trent repeated the number seven for the sacraments, the necessity of the sacraments for salvation, their efficacy "ex opere operato" if no impediment exists, the character impressed by some sacraments, and the necessity of the minister to "do what the Church does."[37]

Professor Jill Raitt wrote her doctoral dissertation at the University of Chicago in 1970. Its title is *The Conversion of the Elements in Reformed Eucharistic Theology with Special Reference to Theodore Beza.* In 1972 she published certain parts of this thesis under the auspices of the American Academy of Religion.[38] In this third chapter I shall quite often refer to this study that has helped me greatly in a voluminous corpus not yet analyzed in a modern way.

In her second chapter, Dr. Raitt underlines the importance of *Confessio Christianae Fidei* which we introduced in this study in the concluding pages of the first section. She explains that de Bèze begins his discussion of the sacraments by relating them to the word, asking why sacraments must be added to the preaching of the word. She shows that in addition to the traditional reasons, de Bèze added that God wanted to stoop to our "crass" human nature still more. He wanted to assure us of the reality

---

37.   Denzinger, nos. 1601-1613.

38.   Raitt, Jill. *The Eucharistic Theology of Theodore Beza*: *Development of the Reformed Doctrine*, A A R Studies in Religion, no. 4. Atlanta, Ga.: Scholars Press, 1976.

of the promise not just in words, but in signs that would engage senses other than hearing. De Bèze uses an example that indicates a theological explanation of sacramental causality:

> For such is their power, whether of the signs or of the rites, that all the senses are drawn to consent to the promises of the Gospel, as if they had been brought into the presence of the thing (res) itself. In a not dissimilar way, if it is permissible to explain the incomprehensible goodness of God in some human similitudes, we see this custom obtaining in many judicial tribunals, so that when some possessions or property is awarded to someone, certain ceremonies are added by which possession is effected. Thus also in civil contracts, even though a notary has signed it and added the names of witnesses, nevertheless, it is customary to affix the seal of the city or of the prince so that the contract will be more valid and authentic.[39]

Interesting for us in this initial section of de Bèze is that, first, through the sacraments, a kind of presence is effected of that signified to the senses. Secondly, a further clue is given with regard to the nature of sacramental causality. The seal of the magistrate is that by which the conveyance of property rights is effected.

With this notion then in mind, de Bèze is able to define what sacraments are in the following way:

> ...certain signs or notes, and visible witnesses constituted by God himself for the perpetual use of the Church on its pilgrimage through this world: and added by the authority of God to the promises of the Gospel of the salvation freely offered by Jesus Christ, so that in this way, he may more efficaciously show to our external senses what he declares to us through the Word, and effects through the Holy Spirit in our

---

39. *Confessio Cristianae Fidei*, pp. 23-24.

Ea enim vis est istorum sive signorum sive rituum, ut omnes sensus non aliter cognatur Evangelii, promissionibus assentiri, quam si in rem ipsam praesentem adducerentur. Non dissimili ratione, se liceat incomprehensam Dei bonitatem humanis quibusdam similitudinibus adumbrare, hunc morem videmus in plerisque iudicum tribulanibus obtinere, ut cum rei cuiuspiam vel dominium, vel possessionem alicui attribuerint, quasdam preterea ceremonias adhibeant quibus ille in possessionem mittatur. Ita etiam in civilibus contractibus, quamvis publicus tabello testium nomina adscripserit, & ipsi instrumento subscripserit: solet tamen civitatis aut principis sigillum apponi, ut prorsus validum & authenticum instrumentum habeatur.

hearts, when he seals that salvation which in this world, we possess only by hope and by faith.[40]

We see here the fundamental Reformed notions of sacraments: sacraments are signs of the promise fulfilled in Christ and given and sealed in the hearts of the faithful through the power of the Spirit. These signs, moreover, are for the use of the Church and make even clearer what is declared in the word.

His next step is to do as did St. Thomas Aquinas. He applies his definition to the sacraments of the Old and New Testaments. The differences are that those of the Old Testament must look forward to an event that has not yet occurred, while those of the New can remember an event that has occurred. God is equally the author of both and participation in Christ the object of both as Paul and Augustine teach.[41]

We find a later text defining the sacraments in the work of de Bèze entitled *Quaestionum et Responsionum, pars altera, quae est de sacramentis*[42] written in 1576. This is a long treatise, instructional rather than polemical in tone. It will be followed by his last effort to conciliate his Lutheran opponents, *De controversiis in Coena Domini* written in 1593.[43]

When de Bèze came to the sign nature of sacraments in his *Questions and Answers*, he made distinctions not found in his earlier works. He

40. *Ibid.*,"...certa nimirum sigma, sive certas notas, ac visibilia testimonia a Deo ipso constituta in perpetuum usum Ecclesia in hoc mundo peregrinantis: & eius auctoritate adiuncta promissionibus Evangelii de gratuita Iesu Christi salute, ut eo efficacius velut nostris externis sensibus demonstraret quod nobis per Verbum declarat, & per Spiritum sanctum in cordibus nostris efficit, quum salutem illam, quam sola spe & fide in hoc mundo possidemus, in cordibus nostris obsignat:..."

41. *Ibid.*, p. 24.

42. Gardy, Frédéric. p. 150f., lists it under the following title: *Quaestionum / et / responsionum/christianarum/pars altera, quae* est de/Sacramentis. /Theodoro Beza/Vezelio, authore. / Aliectus est index/Quaestionum copiosus. /Genevae, /Apud Eustathium Vignon. /M. D. LXXVI. Hereafter referred to as Q. A. It was reprinted in 1577, 1581, 1587, and 1600. Translation of the "pars altera" are fewer than for the first part. Gardy lists nine in French, 1584; one in English, 1580.

43. *De controversiis in Coena Domini, per nonnullos nu per in Germania, partim renovatis, partim, auctis, Christiana et perspicua disceptatio.* Theodore Beza auctore. Genevae, Apud Joannem, le Preux, MDXCIII.

88

affirmed that sacraments are signs of a very particular sort. They are not natural signs, as smoke is the natural sign of fire, nor are they miraculous and prodigious signs as would be signs in the moon and stars. Rather they are made signs by the institution of God and hence belong to the generic category of voluntary signs.[44] Although in sacraments God uses common elements, natural things, their signification is beyond their natural meaning so that what follows the legitimate use of the sacraments is the *Magnum mysterium* spoken of by St. Paul in Ephesians V. Paul is not writing here about the signs themselves, however, but of their effects. Marriage is not a great mystery, but the union of Christ with his Church is a great mystery.[45]

Sacraments differ also from two other voluntary signs of God. Some established by God's command look only to the past and are merely memorials, that is, for example, the twelve stones taken from the Jordan to commemorate the crossing; others appear in the present and carry with them a promise; i.e., the rainbow appears to assure men that God will never again flood the earth. But sacraments touch all three moments of time: past, present and future. While they commemorate a past saving event, they also make present and witness to that which by signifying they offer to us. By doing so, they are pledges and seals of the promise of eternal life.[46]

Once de Bèze had established these general principles, he was ready again to define a sacrament:

> A sacrament is a visible sign divinely instituted for the Church, by the use of which Christ with his benefits regarding eternal life is signified by a certain analogy of correspondence, so that also it is really sealed in the souls of believers.[47]

---

44. *Questions and Answers*, p. 330: 11.

45. *Ibid.*

46. *Ibid.*, p. 331: 12.

47. *Ibid.*, 13. "Sacramentum est signum visibile divinitus Ecclesiae institutum, cuius usu Christus cum suis beneficiis ad vitam aeternam spectantibus ita significatur convenienti quadam analogiam ut etiam reipsa in credentium animis obsignetur."

The Reformer then proceeded to explain the terms of his definitions, and these understandings of his are important for an analysis of his eucharistic doctrine.

A sign may be said to be that which, besides the appearance which bears upon the senses, brings something else to mind to which the sign is analogous.

"Divinely instituted" applies to sacraments in that they are such not by their own nature nor by a miracle but solely by God's institution. The change in them is caused not by saying words, but wholly by God's command expressed by words. In this sense only may the *verba operatoria* be accepted. Here, of course, is a major point of distinction between the Reformer and the Council of Trent. The terms *ex opere operato* and *ex opere operantis* used by St. Thomas Aquinas and incorporated into the documents of the Council of Trent will be unacceptable to the Reformers. We shall not go into a discussion of these terms in this work since it would be too lengthy to develop. Suffice it to say here that this is a basis for the Reformers to deny the nature of the ministerial priesthood and, of course, the sacramental nature of the Mass itself. Based on the teachings of Calvin and de Bèze, this controversy will take on major proportions during the 17th century in France. Remi Snoek has studied the development of this tradition in his dissertation written at Louvain.[48] He writes:

> En ce qui concerne l'Eucharistie, on sait qu'elle avait suscité des débats dès les origines de la Réforme. Nous n'avons pas à nous étendre ici sur les positions adoptées à son égard par les diverses confessions protestantes: elles sont suffisamment connues du lecteur. Rappelons simplement que Calvin, dont la doctrine nous intéresse plus particulièrement, avait adopté une attitude intermédiaire entre celle des luthériens et celle des 'sacramentaires,' quant à la façon de concevoir la présence du Christ au Saint Sacrement.[49]

De Bèze accepted the presence of Christ in the Eucharist as did Calvin. But we see quite clearly that he continued to teach that, though

---

48.   Snoeks, Remi. *L'argument de tradition dans la controverse eucharistique entre catholiques et réformés français au XVIIe siècle.* Louvain: Publications Univeritaires, 1951.

49.   *Ibid.*, pp. 14-15.

Christ was present in the eucharist at the moment of its reception, this presence was not produced by the words pronounced by the priest. Snoek continues:

> Comme on sait, les luthériens, tout en rejetant la transsubstantiation, admettaient la présence réelle du corps du Christ dans le sacrement, au moment de la communion, tandis que les "sacramentaires" prétendaient ne voir dans l'Eucharistie qu'un simple symbole destiné à commémorer notre salut. Or Calvin, conformément à une conception des sacrements qui tend à séparer fortement le signe sensible de la réalité invisible, nie qu'il y ait autre chose dans le signe extérieur que le pain et le vin. Mais, par ailleurs, il enseigne que celui qui prend ces éléments matériels en esprit de foi, participe spirituellement à la substance du corps et du sang du Christ et reçoit ainsi, par l'action du Saint-Esprit, force et vigueur divines. D'autre part, à l'instar des autres réformateurs, il s'oppose résolument à la Messe et reproche aux catholiques, qui la considèrent comme un sacrifice propitiatoire, de déroger par là à la dignité de l'unique immolation du Christ sur la croix. Sa thèse entraîne évidemment la répudiation du culte et des cérémonies eucharistiques de l'Eglise romaine, accusée au surplus de ne pas avoir respecté les préceptes évangéliques concernant la communion sous les deux espèces.[50]

We see then even in this fundamental definition of "sacrament" by de Bèze that the implications in the eucharistic theology of de Bèze are far reaching. His conclusions must coincide with those of Calvin because his starting point and his reasoning are the same.

How did St. Francis de Sales approach this notion of "sacrament"? As always, he took into consideration the teachings of the Council of Trent. The Council had done all the defining that was necessary for him to apply in his own writing. So we see little of the type of theologizing done by St. Thomas

---

50. *Ibid.*, p. 15. "On trouvera, dans la suite, des indications plus détaillées au sujet de la doctrine eucharistique du calvinisme, à propos de l'analyse des ouvrages de certains polémistes réformés ou catholiques." Cf. aussi J. Beckmann, "Vom Sakrament bei Calvin, Die Sakramentslehre Calvins in ihren Beziehung zu Augustin," Tubingue, 1926; J. De Saussure, "Doctrine calviniste des sacrements," *Bulletin de la Société de l'histoire du protestantisme français*, Tome LXXXIV, Paris, 1935, pp. 243-266; W. Niesel, "Calvins Lehre vom Abendmahl," 2ème ed., Munich, 1935; E. Pache, "La sainte Cène selon Calvin," *Revue de Théologie et de philosophie* t. XXIV, Lausanne, 1936, p. 308-327; J. Cadier, *La présence réele dans le calvinisme, Etudes théologiques et religieuses*, t. XIII, Montpellier, 1938, p. 293-309; H. Grass, *Die Abendmahislehre bei Luther und Calvin. Eine kritische Untersuchung*, Gutersloh, 1940.

in the Tertia Pars of the *Summa Theologica* (Questions 60-65). We already know of Francis' thorough familiarity with these Thomistic teachings and his attitude towards their implementation in the Tridentine documents. One sees rather the practical application of these principles themselves in his writings which he composed to refute the teachings of the Reformers. A major work of Francis in the Counter-Reform was the *Controversies*. Actually, St. Francis himself did not use the term for these particular polemical writings. He calls them his *Meditations*. But Dom Mackey explains in his Preface the use of this term:

> Tous les éditeurs des *Oeuvres de saint François de Sales* ont désigné sous le nom de 'Controverses' l'Oeuvre polémique dont nous traitons actuellement. Ce nom, accepté dans cette Préface, est en effet bien choisi et propre à représenter le caractère de l'ouvrage de l'Apôtre du Chablais, en montrant ses points de contact avec les 'Controversiae' de Bellarmin. Cependant, pour approfondir la nature de ce traité il faut rappeler les diverses dénominations que son saint Auteur lui donne. Jamais il ne désigne ces feuilles sous le nom de 'Controverses'; ainsi qu'on l'a dit plus haut, il les appelle quelquefois ses "Meditations"; toutefois, le nom dont il se sert dans l'ouvrage même est celui de "Memorial."[51]

Francis manifests his attitude towards the Reformers when he writes the following:

> Ce mot de Sacrement est bien expres en l'Escriture en la signification qu'il a en l'Eglise Catholique, puysque saint Pol, parlant du Mariage, l'apelle clair et net, "Sacrement." Mays nous (allons) voir cecy cy apres; il suffit maintenant, contre l'insolence de Zuingle et autres qui ont voulu rejetter ce nom, que toute l'Eglise ancienne en aye usé: car ce n'est pas avec une plus grand'authorité que le mot de Trinité, Consubstantiel, Personne, et cent autres sont demeurés en l'Eglise comme saints et legitimes; et c'est une tres inutile et sotte temerité de vouloir changer les motz ecclesiastiques que l'antiquité nous a laissé, outre le danger quil y auroit, qu'apres le changement des motz en n'allast au change de l'intelligence et creance, comme on voit ordinayrement que c'est l'intention de ces novateurs de paroles.[52]

---

51. *Oeuvres*. I, p. CXIX.

52. *Ibid.*, p. 350.

In order that Francis write this way, he had to be very familiar with the teaching of the Council of Trent. Beginning with the Session VII in 1547 and extending to the Session XXIV in 1563, the Council had treated the doctrines taught by Luther. These, in turn, would find acceptance in part in the teachings of John Calvin. We have seen how Théodore de Bèze was faithful to the teachings of his master. Now we see that in the reiteration of Calvin's teachings within de Bèze's writings, there is somewhat of a reexpression and more scholastic presentation of the first generation of Reformers.

Francis reacted to the Reformers' sacramental positions in full awareness of the content of the Council's decisions from Session VII in 1547. When the Council teaches: "Si quis dixerit, sacramenta novae Legis non fuisse omnia Jesu Christo Domino nostro instituta, aut esse plura vel pauciora, quam septem, videlicet baptismum, confirmationem, Eucharistiam, paenitentiam, extremam unctionem, ordinem et matrimonium, aut etiam aliquod horum septem non esse vere et proprie sacramentum, anathema sit,"[53] it is replying to the Reformers' statements. St. Francis knew as well the Canon 6 that taught the following:

> If anyone says that the sacraments of the New Law do not contain the grace which they signify or that they do not confer that grace on those who do not place an obstacle in the way, as if they were only external signs of the grace or justice received through faith and a kind of mark of the Christian profession by which among men the faithful are distinguished from the unbelievers, anathema sit.[54]

Because of the Council's teachings and his own fidelity to them, Francis was able to write and preach to his flock on the sacramental order in the following way:

> Avant que sçavoir comment il nous faut preparer pour recevoir les Sacremens et quel fruict nous en devons tirer, il est necessaire de sçavoir que c'est que Sacrements et leurs effects. Les Sacremens doncques sont des canaux par lesquels, pour

---

53.   Denzinger, H. et Schönmetzer, A. *Enchiridion Symbolorum - Definitionum et Decretionum de Rebus et Morum*. Herder, Friburgi Brisgoviae, 1963, p. 382.

54.   Meuner, J. and Dupuis, J. *The Christian Faith in the Doctrinal Documents of the Catholic Church*. New York: Alba House, 1981, p. 371.

ainsi parler, Dieu descend à nous, comme par l'oraison nous montons à luy, puisque l'oraison n'est autre chose qu'une elevation de nostre esprit en Dieu. Les effects des Sacramens sont divers, quoy qu'ils n'ayent tous qu'une mesme fin et pretention, qui est de nous unir à Dieu....[55]

This citation is drawn from *Les vrays entretiens spirituels* which is a collection of 21 conferences given by St. Francis to his Visitandines in the yard of the Gallery at Annecy. They were intended as a type of group spiritual direction in the early years of the existence of the Visitation community. This type of understanding of the Church's teaching regarding the nature of the sacraments is very necessary in the Salesian system of asceticism. The rest of this "Conference" develops the elementary notion of the nature and the effects of the sacraments and then applies it to all the seven sacraments within the Roman Church. We have seen already that such a notion is present in his doctrine on the Eucharist. It will be very important in his teaching regarding the nature of the Eucharist as sacrifice.

2.   Transubstantiation:

After dealing with the sacraments in general, de Bèze deals with the Lord's Supper. Here, under signs, he names the bread and wine, blessed by the minister *ex Dei verbo*, and under ceremonies or essential ritual actions, the breaking and distributing and the consuming of the elements. The *res* of this sacrament, like that of Baptism, is Christ, the historical, risen Christ. The identity of the Christ present is therefore established: there is only one Christ who was born, suffered, died, rose from the dead, and ascended into heaven, and who now incorporates the faithful into his body spiritually by faith. Therefore, it is perfectly legitimate to speak of the true body and blood of Christ in reference to the sacrament of the Lord's Supper. Through the Holy Spirit, the body and blood of Christ are as truly offered to faith as the bread and wine are offered to the senses.[56]

Théodore de Bèze then discusses the application of the names of the body and blood to the elements which may be done symbolically. His examples are the cup which is symbolically called the testament, as was

55.   *Oeuvres*, VI, p. 337.

56.   *Confessio Christianae Fidei*, p. 30.

circumcision in the Old Law. In like manner, the Lamb is called the Passover, and the rock, Christ. Thus Paul can call the bread the communion (koinonia) of the body of Christ and the cup the communion of the blood of Christ. All equally efficaciously represent Christ, even though in the case of the Old Testament sacraments, he was not yet born in the flesh.[57] The trope, or symbolical language used here is justified by de Bèze as belonging to Scripture, not to the originality of the Reformed theologians. He even testifies to its antiquity by quoting Virgil and Homer.[58]

Our theologian is just beginning, in this *Confession*, to elaborate his understanding and use of the term *analogia*. He explains the analogy of the sign and the signified in three ways: 1) the breaking of the bread represents the suffering of the Lord; 2) the distribution of the bread teaches in a sensible manner that Christ and all his benefits are given to each individual; 3) the bread made from many grains and the wine made from many grapes signifies the union of all the members in the one body of Christ and the mutual charity they should exercise toward one another. His use of analogy is here drawn from scriptural examples[59] rather than from philosophical principles. But his use of the term "analogy" in his definition will require him to explain the role it plays not only in the sacramental rites, but also in the understanding and defense of those rites as effective instruments of the Holy Spirit.

Towards this end, de Bèze begins to draw together the doctrines of the agency of the Spirit, the instrumentality of faith, and incorporation into Christ:

---

57.   *Ibid.*, pp. 30-31. "Usitatum enim est, quam de Sacramentis agitur, ad declarandam sacramentalis significationis efficaciam ad veritatem, symbolis attribuere rerum ipsarum nominae. Sic enim dicitur poculum esse novum testamentum, id est, verum & certum symbolum novi testamenti, quod effusione sanguinis Iesu Christi sancitum est. Sic Circumcisio vocatur foedus, id est, verum foederis pignus. Sic alicubi Agnus dicitur esse Pascha: Petra deserti Christus, quod Christum vere & efficaciter repraesentarent, quamvis eius caro nondum in rerum natura estaret: adeo certa est rerum etiam absentium praesentia, quae verbo Dei & fide nititur:..."

58.   *Ibid.*, p. 31.

59.   Cf., critical notes of Réveillaud, p. 86.

By the fact that we receive and eat the bread, and drink from the cup, we are assured that Jesus Christ is truly communicated to us, as we said before. For the Holy Spirit knows how to join closely, by the bond of faith, those things which, according to spatial distance, are very far apart. Therefore, as we receive the natural symbols in a natural way, and eat and drink them, so that by the power of the natural faculty, they are united with our substance, thus also, in a heavenly and spiritual mode, Jesus Christ, who according to the flesh is now in heaven and nowhere else, is truly communicated to us, so that we are flesh of his flesh and bone of his bone; that is, so that we are made one with Christ and inserted into his body through faith, whence we draw eternal life.[60]

This comprehensive statement is a fitting conclusion to the preacher's exposition of the Lord's Supper; it indicates the direction his development of the notion of analogy will take and also its importance to help his readers grasp something of the nature of sacramental efficacy. This is not so much explained by the type of causality that operates juridically when a seal is affixed to a document, but rather the connection between sacrament and life in Christ, between sign and signified, is drawn close in the analogy of food and drink, the sustenance of life itself.

De Bèze had already given his notion of the Lord's Supper at the Colloquy of Poissy when he addressed the Cardinal of Lorraine in the following terms:

The bread which we break according to his (God's) institution, is the communication of the true body of Jesus Christ which was delivered up for us: and the cup we drink, is the communication of the true blood shed for us, that is to say, in that same substance which he took from the womb of the virgin Mary and which he bore into heaven. And I beg you, sirs, in the name of God, what could you then look for or find in this holy Sacrament, that we too do not look for and find there?[61]

---

60.   *Confessio Christianae Fidei*, p. 31. "Quod autem panem accipimus & ex poculo bibimus, restatur Iesum Christum vere nobis communicari, sicut antea diximus. Novit enim Spiritus sanctus arctissime coniungere fidei vinculo, quae aliqui, si locorum distantiam spectes, longissime sunt dissita. Quemaddum (sic) igitur naturali modo accipimus, edimus & bibimus naturalia symbola, quae postea virtute naturalis facultatis in nostram substantiam coalescunt: ita etiam caelesti: & spirituali modo Iesus Christus, qui nunc est in caelis & non alibi secundum carnem, vere nobis communicatur, ut simus caro ex carne eius, & ossa ex ipsius ossibus, id est, ut cum Christo unum facti, & insiti eius corpori per fidem, vitam aeternam inde hauriamus:..."

61.   Cf., Raitt, J., p. 34. "Que le pain que nous rompons selon son ordonnance, est la communication du vray corps de Iesus Christ qui a este livré pour nous: et la coupe dont nous

What the assembled Catholic prelates, theologians and royalty wanted to hear was "transubstantiation" or "consubstantiation." But, pleaded de Bèze, this concept is directly contrary to the analogy and agreement of our faith since it contradicts the very nature of a sacrament which is to be a *SIGN* of the substance of the body and blood of Christ. "Consubstantiation" and "transubstantiation" were dismissed by de Bèze as non-scriptural and unnecessary.[62]

The Council of Trent in its Session XIII defined the notion of "transubstantiation" in its fourth chapter in the following way:

> Quoniam autem Christus redemptor noster corpus suum id, quod sub specie panis offerebat (cf. Mt 26, 26 ss; Mc 14, 22 ss; Lc 22, 19 s; 1 Cor 11, 24 ss.), vere esse dixit, ideo persuasum semper in Ecclesia Dei fuit, idque nunc denuo sancta haec Synodus declarat: per consecrationem panis et vini conversionem fieri totius substantiae panis in substantiam corporis Christi Domini nostri, et totius substantiae vini in substantiam sanguinis eius. Quae conversio convenienter et proprie a sancta catholica Ecclesia transsubstantiatio est appellata (can. 2).[63]

Francis de Sales uses this Tridentine notion which was absolutely unacceptable to Théodore de Bèze in any number of instances; for example, in a lenten sermon Francis speaks of the resurrection of the dead. He questions himself on how this rising of the dead will take place:

> Mais comment se fait cecy? Par la vertu de la parole de Dieu. Alors nous verrons cet admirable miracle de la transsubstantiation qui s'opere tous les jours au Sacrement de l'Eucharistie...[64]

Francis de Sales was following the teachings of the Angelic Doctor who had used the terms "transubstantiatio" or one of its forms many times in

---

buvons, est la communication du vray sang qui a esté respandu pour nous: voire, en ceste mesme substance qu'il a emportee d'avec nous au ciel. Et je vous prie, Messieurs, au nom de Dieu, que pouvez vous doncques chercher ni trouver en ce sainct Sacrement, que nous n'y cherchions et trouvions aussi?"

62. *Ibid.*, p. 699.

63. Denzinger, p. 387.

64. *Oeuvres*, X. p. 315.

his writings. The following table will show from the *Index thomisticus* by Robert Busa that this term was used 78 times in the *Sentences* and five times in the *Summa Theologica*. The abbreviation equivalents can be read in the work itself.[65]

The frequent recurrence of the terms "transubstantiation" and "consubstantiation" would have made this concept foremost in the minds of both Francis and Théodore de Bèze. Their respective positions were taken in full light of the importance of this notion and of those doctrines stemming from it.

	ISN	4SN	RIC	RIL	QDL	ST 4	AUT
transubstantiatio	0	21	1	4	3	3	1
transubstantione	0	10				2	1
transubstantionem	0	19		1	3		1
transubstantionis	1	8		1	1		
transubstantio	2	17	1	1	1		
(1 conj)							
TOTAL	3+	75	=	78 (*Sentences*)			
				5 (*Summa Theologica*)			
				83 (S + ST) = Total			

Summa Theologica

00026	75.4 co/42
00027	75.8 co/38
00028	78.5 aql/7
00043	78.1 co/18
00059	78.4 co/3
	others
00029	(QDP) 6.2.ra2/4
00045	(OS2) 31.ag/2
00006	(REM) 14.2/392

The following would be one of the better known of the Angelic Doctor's texts because of its explicit nature and direct statement of the

---

65.   Busa, Robert. *Index Thomisticus - Sancti Thomae Aquinatis operum Omnium Indicus et Concordantiae.* Stuttgart-Bad Canstatt: Fromann-Holzboog, 1974. Vol. 22, pp. 373-374.

substantial change that takes place at the transubstantiation in the Mass. The Council of Trent used this text in its definition of Church doctrine:

> Respondum dicendum quod, sicut supra (6) dictum est, cum in hoc sacramento sit verum corpus Christi, nec incipiat ibi esse de novo per motum localem; cum etiam nec corpus Christi..sit ibi sicut in loco, ut ex dictis (7) patet; necesse est dicere quod ibi incipiat esse per conversionem substantiae panis in ipsu. Haec tamen conversio non est similis conversionibus naturalibus, sed est omnino supernaturalis, sola Dei virtute effecta....

Thomas Aquinas then cites St. Ambrose, St. John the Evangelist and St. John Chrysostom as authorities who support his argument. Then he continues:

> Manifestum est enim quod omne agens agit in quantum est actu. Quodlibet autem agens creatum est determinatum in suo actu: cum sit determinati generis et speciei. Et ideo cuiuslibet agentis creati actio fertur super aliquem determinatum actum. Determinatio autem cuiuslibet rei in esse actuali est per eius formam. Unde nullum agens naturale vel creatum potest agere nisi ad immutationem formae. Et propter hoc omnis conversio quae fit secundum leges naturae, est formalis. Sed Deus est infinitus actus, ut in Prima Parte (8) habitum est. Unde eius actio se extendit ad totam naturam entis. Non igitur solum potest perficere conversionem formalem, ut scilicet diversae formae sibi in eodem subiecto succedant: sed conversionem totius entis, ut scilicet tota substantia huius convertatur in totam substantiam illius. Et hoc agitur divina virtute in hoc sacramento. Nam tota substantia panis convertitur in totam substantiam corporis Christi, et tota substantia vini in totam substantiam sanguinis Christi. Unde haec conversio non est formalis, sed substantialis. Nec continetur inter species motus naturalis, sed proprio nomine potest dici transubstantiatio.

> (6)   Art. 2
> (7)   Q. 1, ad 2.
> (8)   Q.7, a.1; q. 25, a.2.[66]

3.   Mass as Sacrifice:

The use of the teachings of St. Thomas Aquinas by the Council of Trent and their implementation by this student of Aquinas and Bishops of

66.   Aquinas, Thomas. *Summa Theologica*, Marietti, Romae, 1948, IIIa Pars., Q. 75, a. 4 (c), p. 500.

the Council, provokes the following type of statement in the most fundamental of Salesian books, the *Introduction of the Devout Life*:

> Je ne vous ay encor point parlé du soleil des exercices spirituelz, qui est le tressaint, sacré et tres souverain Sacrifice et Sacrement de la Messe, centre de la religion chrestienne, coeur de la devotion, ame de la pieté, mystere ineffable qui comprend l'abisme de la charité divine, et par lequel Dieu s'appliquant reellement a nous, nous communique magnifiquement ses graces et faveurs.[67]

This passage manifests the importance of the Thomistic and Tridentine sense of the "sacraments" themselves; it further implies Francis' adhesion to the doctrines of the priesthood of the Mass and the many theological implications that depend upon this interpretation of the importance in the Christian life of faith, the Mass and the Eucharist itself. This faith and practice we find fundamental in a more recent theologian who states in capsule form that which Francis understood so well. Henri De Lubac writes:

> Mais si le sacrifice est accepté de Dieu, si la prière de l'Eglise est exaucée, c'est qu'à son tour, au sens le plus strict, *l'Eucharistie FAIT l'Eglise*. Elle est, nous dit saint Augustin, le sacrement *quo in hoc tempore consociatur Ecclesia*.[68] Elle achève l'oeuvre que le baptême avait commencée. *Ex latere Christi dormientis in cruce sacramenta profluxerunt, quibus Ecclesia fabricatur*.[69] Déjà "nous avons été baptisés en un seul Esprit, pour former un seul Corps."[70] Voici maintenant que ce Corps, en chacun des membres que nous sommes, reçoit même nourriture et même breuvage, pour entretenir sa vie et parfaire son unité.[71] *Perficiamur in corpore*.[72]

In this statement we find stated the Roman Catholic notion of the implications of the "transubstantiation": the Mass, and the real presence in

---

67. *Oeuvres*, III, p. 100.

68. Mopsueste, Théodore de. *Seizième homélie catéchétique*, p. 531. Theodore of Mupsuestia, *Sixteenth Cathetical Homily*, Tonneau-Devresse, Città del Vaticano, 1939, p. 129.

69. John XIX, 34. Cf. Aquinas, *Summa*, IIIa Pars., Q. 64, a. 2, ad 3 m.

70. 1 Corinthians XII, 13. Cf. Aquinas, *Summa*. IIIa Pars, Q. 39, a. 6, ad. 4 m.

71. Aquinas, *Summa*, Q. 73, a 3.

72. De Lubac, Henri. *Méditations sur l'église*. Paris: Aubier. p. 129.

the Eucharist itself and especially the notion of the Eucharist as sacrifice.
How different is all this from the Reformers' notions which Théodore de
Bèze presented at Poissy when he declared:

> Mais il nous semble, selon la petite mesure de cognoissance
> que nous avons receue de Dieu, que ceste transubstantiation
> ne se rapporte à l'analogie et convenance de nostre foy,
> d'autant qu'elle est directement contraire à la nature des
> sacremens, esquels il faut necessairement que les signes
> substantiels demeurent, pour estre vrais signes de la substance
> du corps et du sang de Jesus Christ, et est pareillement
> renversée la verité de la nature humaine et ascension d'iceluy.
> Je dy le semblable de la seconde opinion qui est de la
> Consubstantiation, laquelle outre tout cela n'ha nul fondement
> sur les paroles de Jesus Christ, et n'est aucunement necessaire
> à ce que nous soyons participans du fruict des sacremens.[73]

The Reformers' interpretation verbalized by de Bèze before the
French court and ecclesiastical dignitaries, when applied in a theological
sense, directly contradicts a whole series of Roman teachings such as the
Eucharist as sacrifice.

We have already touched on the teaching of de Sales relative to the
Eucharist as sacrifice. When he writes: "celui qui dirait que le sacrifice de la
Messe et celui de la Croix sont deux sacrifices, dirait vrai...."[74] He is
following the teachings of the theologians and the Councils of the Church.

On the other hand, Kilian McDonnell in his wonderful thesis points
out that:

> In a passage remarkable for its sacrificial orientation Calvin
> upholds the unity between the sacrifice of the cross and the
> eucharistic memorial of that sacrifice, a memorial brought
> about by the figures or signs of bread and wine. We are so
> grafted into Christ, so united to him that the sacrifice which he
> offered belongs to us as though we had ourselves offered it.[75]

He continues to write in a very understanding manner the following
observation:

---

73. Baum, G., I. p. 573.

74. *Oeuvres*, XXIII, p. 105.

75. McDonnell, Kilian. *John Calvin, the Church and the Eucharist*. Princeton, N.J.:
Princeton Press, 1967, p. 284.

It is possible to construct a rather remarkable theology of sacrifice from texts, and not isolated texts, from Calvin's writings. Such a theology would not invalidate the polemic Calvin directed against the Roman theology of sacrifice. But it would be totally misleading to think that this more positive approach to sacrifice is characteristic of Calvin's eucharistic teaching. The texts are there, as are the beginnings of a more complete theology of sacrifice as applied to the Eucharist, but they are left undeveloped, and they stand on the periphery of Calvin's eucharistic preoccupations, possibly because of the strong stand he felt he must take against the Roman position.[76]

How true was such a "strong stand" on the part of Théodore de Bèze in being faithful to his mentor? After an exposition on how he explains why the Holy Spirit is called the Paraclete or comforter, Jill Raitt writes the following:

If nothing remained of de Bèze's eucharistic works except this section of *Confessio*, he would deserve the title of Calvin's epigone for there is nothing in this little treatise which is not also in Calvin's writing on the Lord's Supper. But de Béze's effort to define indicates a tendency to systematize which differs from Calvin's fluent exegesis and discursive humanism.[77]

Did the following text come from de Bèze as a part of a forceful pronouncement of his religious beliefs or rather as an effort to be "Calvin's epigone"? He writes:

La chose du Sacrement, c'est à dire Jesus Christ, est recue de nous en manière spirituelle, par la Foy. Or appellons-nous manière spirituelle de recevoir ou de communier, non point celle par laquelle l'esprit du Christ seulement nous est communiqué, mais celle qui n'est aucunement terrestre ou naturelle, ains dépend de la puissance incomprehensible du Sainct Esprit, qui est le lieu très étroit et serré; par lequel les membres de plus en plus font lier avecques le corps.[78]

We believe he is in the preceding text a faithful follower of his predecessor. But we likewise believe that he followed Calvin in his effort to

---

76. *Ibid.*, p. 285.

77. Raitt, J. p. 30.

78. Bèze, Théodore de. *Vray et droite intelligence de ces paroles de la Saincte Cène de Jesus Christ, Cecy est mon corps, & Traitte...*fait en latin par M. Th. de Bèze, et traduit en françois par M. Louis des Masures, à Metz, Jean d'Arras, & Odinet, Baffont, 1564. p. 82.

refute that which was the Roman Church's position. In one of his more vituperative moments he wrote:

> Le vin aussi offert en leurs calices Missaux, transubstantié en sang, le vin n'était plus vin: mais un accident sans substance. Y eut-il jamais magie plus abominable, et heresie plus détestable que cette transubstantiation Messaliane...?[79]

In what kind of age was such a text written? To what had the times and customs led such a man who followed so idealistic a leader as John Calvin? In his chapter dealing with Calvin's successors and their treatment of "La sainte cène". . .Jean Cadier writes at the end of the section he devotes to Théodore de Bèze:

> Echec dans son effort de conciliation avec les luthériens, échec dans son effort de conciliation avec les catholiques, ces deux échecs de Théodore de Bèze, si douloureux soient-ils, ne le diminuent pas. Au cours de ces débats, avec une maîtrise remarquable de la parole et de la pensée, il a précisé la doctrine calviniste. Maintenant la présence dans la gloire de la personne humaine du Christ, il affirme l'action du Saint-Esprit pour accorder dans la foi la présence vivifiante du Sauveur dans le pain et le vin de la Cène. Et le réformé qui, sans se décourager, poursuivra à notre époque des entretiens sur la Cène avec des frères d'autres confessions pourra leur adresser l'adjuration de Bèze: 'Et je vous prie, Messieurs, au nom de Dieu, que pouvez-vous donc chercher ni trouver en ce saint sacrement que nous n'y cherchions et trouvions aussi?'[80]

And the ecumenical dialogue continues!!!

---

79.   Bèze, Théodore de. *Sommaire recueil des signes sacrez, sacrifices, et sacramens instituez de Dieu depuis la création du monde. Et de la vraye origine du sarifice de la Messe.* 1561, p. 177.

80.   Cadier, J. p. 109.

CONCLUSION

At the time of this writing, it is certainly not our place to add to the "argumentation" of the 16th and 17th centuries. Rather it is our task to understand the positions of the people involved, the climate of the times and the means they took to resolve their differences. The importance of the Eucharist remains much the same to each of the groups represented by Théodore de Bèze and Francis de Sales. They use this sacrament as the means of expressing their faith in the risen Christ. Both believe in the real presence. They each believe the Eucharist as memorial. The theological shift to an anthropological approach to God was brought about by the humanistic Renaissance in which each of our protagonists was completely immersed. Given the Reformed theology, there could be no agreement on the nature of sacrament, the Mass as sacrifice, the transubstantiation and other doctrines and practices that had been the very basis of Roman Catholic dogma. To really come to a complete and integral understanding of this period is extremely difficult given the complexities and the nature of historiography. Protestant and Catholic narrations are markedly different. The "Christian Institutions" were an inspirational source for the doctrines of Théodore de Bèze. Calvin wrote them in order to bring about the purification that he, as Luther, was convinced was necessary within the Church. De Bèze remained faithful to his master in his dogmatic teaching. Geisendorf states very clearly: "... dans le domaine du dogme par exemple, et peut-être par conscience de son infériorité vis-à-vis de son maître, il n'a jamais rien voulu changer à l'oeuvre de Calvin...".[1] This, of course, does not mean that de Bèze was inferior in his abilities as a leader of the second generation Reformers. Certainly his gifts in the domain of politics and church management were superior to those of Calvin. This is also eminently true of his capability of directing the new university in Geneva. He was an academic. By training, Calvin was also an academic. However, their importance to each other has made it necessary here to study Calvin's doctrine to know his follower's.

Each man was a student of St. Augustine. They realized that the Eucharist was the means of regaining the intimate presence of Christ in the believer's interior life. That is why we have presented an analysis of *La confession de foi du chrétien*. We find here a restatement of the eucharistic doctrine of Calvin to which Théodore de Bèze struggled to remain faithful. After a life of struggle against the Catholic teaching of the Eucharist, de Bèze wrote his very last polemical work on the Eucharist: namely, the *De controversiis in Coena Domini...* in 1593. From that moment, Théodore will write poetry and other literary works. But he will no longer compose any doctrinal work of a controversial nature.

Both Calvin and de Bèze understood that the Eucharist gave the possibility to believers to live in fraternal charity. They both taught that Jesus Christ was the bread of life who had descended from heaven for mankind. The plenitude of life could be found in his humanity. In rejecting the doctrine of transubstantiation and that of the ubiquity of the body of Christ, the Reformers were at the very center of their doctrine. Just how is the communion with Christ brought about? In order to participate in the body of Christ, who is in heaven, it would be improper to bring down to the level of man that which was incorruptible or to imagine that He was omnipresent. It is at this point where the Reformers introduced the role of the third person of the Trinity. It is the Holy Spirit who joins us in Christ. It is in the Spirit that we are made one with Him in spirit, soul and body. It is by the Spirit that we are joined and that all that Christ possesses descends to us.

---

1.   *Op. cit.*, p. 261.

Théodore de Bèze accepted the distinction between the exterior sign and the spiritual substance, but he did not want to separate the one from the other. For him, as for Calvin, when the sign is given us, so also is the substance given us. The sign of the breaking of the bread is not artificial because the truth of Him who is there represented is conjoined. So it is then that in the reception of the sign of the body of Christ, the communicant actually receives the body of Christ.

The Reformers refute the doctrine of transubstantiation or consubstantiation in saying that the bread must be separate from the wine, the body from the blood or inversely. So de Bèze rejects the doctrine of concomitance according to which the blood is in the body and the body is likewise in the blood. This refutation is based on the distinction between the signs and the things represented. We must look for Christ in heaven in the glory of his kingdom. This is the only manner in which we can be nourished by His body and blood under the signs of bread and wine. We can very clearly see by glancing at the writing of Théodore de Bèze that he wrote more on the Eucharist than on any other subject. It involved a more scholarly approach than Calvin's, but was not more innovative. We have tried to show that his familiarity with St. Augustine brought him and Calvin close together. However, the familiarity of de Bèze with the Thomistic writings of the *Contra Gentiles* and the *Summa Theologica* enabled him to present the doctrine in a more scholastic way. The time element is very important at this point. De Bèze was able to refute the early Reformers. At the Colloquy of Poissy, he manifested his detailed knowledge of Trent's teachings. Though St. Thomas Aquinas himself would have taught many of these doctrines in the 12th century, the Church did not implement them universally until the 16th. The writings of Théodore de Bèze serve as a link among the early Reformers, the Council of Trent and the evolution of the Protestant movement into the 17th century.

In a lovely letter from de Bèze to Calvin, we see the very polished disciple politically representing his esteemed mentor at the court of France. He wrote this from St-Germain-en-Laye on August 25, 1561. He greets Calvin with "Monsieur et père". After a rather lengthy description of his reception at court by the king, queen and cardinals, the trusted legate states:

"Adonc le Cardinal prenant la parole, et commenceant par belles louanges, adjousta qu'ainsy que j'avoys affligé la France, je la pourroys maintenant soulager. Je ne lui laissay passer ce mot d'affliction, de sorte qu'il ne mist guieres à changer propos. On m'enquist de vostre age, estat, etc. Je respondy ce qui en est. On se pleind des livres diffamatoires; je ne fus desgarny de juste et veritable defense."[2] This is a typical example of a part of one of many frank and candid reports to his mentor. De Bèze greets his master with warmth and cordiality. He often closes with "tuus", but in this missive he closes with "Vostre entier et humble filz en nostre Seigneur". Actually he uses a pseudonym this time: T. De Chalonay.

The letter describes further a theological discussion with the Cardinal of Lorraine and other prelates of the Roman Church. De Bèze, after a brief description of this encounter writes: "Cependant noz theologiens disputent de la moustarde, et son bien empeschez, comme l'on dict. Mais sy avons nous bien besoin de prier nostre Dieu, plustost que de croire ceulx qui nous les font si contemptibles. ...Si Dieu faisoit ce bien à son église de vous y veoir, alors oseroys-je bien esperer certaine victoire et le plus grand bien qui jamais advint à ce royaume."[3] Théodore de Bèze était a talented and faithful transmitter and developer of the dogmatic and theological teachings (the Eucharist included) of Jean Calvin.

As we have tried to show in this study, Francis de Sales was no less a talented and faithful transmitter of the Church's Tridentine teachings. He presents and develops for us a very classical Catholic concept of the eucharistic doctrine. However, his teachings in other areas of spiritual and mystical theology reveal an individual who, like de Bèze, had his own genius and exercised it in a way that was original and constructive for his Church and her adherents.

Francis' use of scripture is less didactic than that of Calvin or de Bèze. His was a more rhetorical approach. He was trying to lead his religious or faithful to an implementation of his asceticism in their daily lives. It was not

---

2.   Dufour, A. *Correspondance*, III, p. 135.

3.   *Ibid.*, p. 136.

being used as a basis for teaching, but rather as an *argumentum ex auctoritate*. This is often true also in his teachings dealing with the Eucharist. He was seeking to reinforce the traditional teachings of the Church and particularly those set down in the documents of the Council of Trent.

Trained in law and in theology in Paris and Padua, de Sales was very accustomed to the scholastic style of presentation. However, since his readers and listeners were not being initiated into a drastically new way of religious thought, he did not often invoke a syllogistic type of approach. His listeners enjoyed a confidence in his that would be "rarissime" among French believers today. His own absolute confidence and trust in the "total deposit" of truth contained in the Roman Catholic Church and her teachings provoked his very positive and traditional doctrine of the Eucharist. To understand the faith and mode of action of this man is to understand his statement that he is "only a child of his times".[4]

His positions regarding the Reformed doctrines, and for the purpose of this study, that of the Eucharist in particular, demand a good understanding of the historical, religious, philosophical and civilization aspects of the place and time in which he lived. He was often intolerant in his approach to the Protestants in the diocese where he worked. Ruth Kleinman was the first to study this question objectively and to show that, in effect, Francis was not always the "gentleman saint" as he is often pictured by the writers of the 17th and 18th centuries. On the contrary, he was the son of aristocrats. He resented the democratic teachings of the Huguenots. The king was king of God's will. That which interfered with the success of the monarchy was reproachable. He cooperated with the Duke of Savoy in his campaigns to retake Geneva into the duchy. Francis did seek refuge in the Allinges while working as a missionary in the Chablais. He did identify with those who were not at all God's poor and miserable; he was a "child of his times".[5]

---

4.   *Oeuvres*, VI, p. 216.

5.   *Ibid.*

The Eucharistic teaching of Francis de Sales is throughout his writings. It plays a very important part in his method of spirituality. The approach of Théodore de Bèze was more of an academic who presented formally developed treatises on precise subjects. Francis was a very busy missionary early in his priesthood. Then he became an even busier bishop-pastor. The traces of his genius are found much more in the presentation of his doctrine in the *Treatise on the Love of God* and other works in a humanistic manner. His ineffable quality of describing the spiritual operation of the soul in its state of seeking union with God is one rarely found among writers in the history of the world. The place of the Eucharist in this God-centered doctrine is fundamental. For this reason, the teaching of the Eucharist is found throughout the many volumes, sermons, letters and opuscules that make up the Salesian corpus. This sacrament of love gives the lover an excellent occasion to be united on earth with the one loved. How important is this constituent of an ascetic system based on spiritual progress!

Both Théodore de Bèze and Francis de Sales taught doctrines of the Eucharist. These doctrines, different as they may be, were presented by two men comparably gifted. Their teachings, passed to us, exemplify this. Would that our lives profit from these exemplary models of faith and teachings!

BIBLIOGRAPHY

SOURCES

Bèze, Théodore de. *Ad repetitionem primam F. Claudii de Sainctes. De rebus Eucharistiae controversis.* Théodori Bezae responsio, Genevae, apud Eusthatium Vignon, 1577, 102 p.

_____. *Adversus Sacramentariorum errorem pro vera Christi praesentia in Coena Domini.* homiliae duae, auctore Nathanaele Nesekio (pseud.) 71 p. Theopoli (S.E.), 1574.

_____. *Chrestiennes meditations sur huict pseaumes du prophete David.* Composees et nouvellement mises en lumiere par Theodore de Besze. Fleuron, tête d'ange entre deux cornes d'abondance - MDLXXXIII.

_____. *Correspondance de Théodore de Bèze:* recueillie par Hippolyte et Béatrice Nicollier. Société du Musée Historique de la Réformation, 13 vols. parus, Genève: Librairie Droz, 1960.

_____. *De coena Domini, plena et perspicua tractatio, in qua Joachimi Westphali calumniae postremum editae refelluntur.* Oliva Roberta Stephani. 1559.

_____. *La seconde partie des questions et responses chrestiennes, en laquelle est amplement traité des Sacramens tant en general qu'en particulier.* Chez Eustace Vignon, 1584.

Bèze, Théodore de, et Marot, Clement. *Les psaumes de David mis en rime françaises.* Genève: Paul Marceau, 1626, in 40.

Bèze, Théodore de. *Opéra.* Genève, 1560.

_____. *Pro corporis Christi veritate.* 1581.

_____. *Sommaire déclaration de Th. de Bèze sur certains points par lui proposés en assemblées des cardineaux et evesques de France et des ministres de l'Eglise.* (Poissy) le six sept. 1561.

_____. *Sommaire recueil des signes sacrez, sacrifices, et sacramens instituez de Dieu depuis la création du monde. Et de la vraye origine du sacrifice de la Messe.* 1561.

_____. *Tractationum theologicarum volumen alterum.* in-fol. Genève: Vignon, 1573.

_____. *Vray et droite intelligence de ces paroles de la Saincte Cène de Jesus Christ, Cecy est mon corps, & Traitte*...fait en latin par M. Th. de Bèze, et traduit en français par M. Louis des Masures, a Metz, Jean d'Arras, & Odinet, Baffont, 1564.

Calvin, John. *Institutes of the Christian Religion.* (Vol. I., Beveridge Translation.) Grand Rapids, Mich: Eerdman, 1983.

François de Sales. *Oeuvres:* Edition complète...publiée par Dom Henry Bernard Mackey et par les soins des Religieuses de la Visitation du ler Monastère d'Annecy. 27 vol. Annecy: Niérat, 1892-1964.

STUDIES

1. General

Baudrillart, Alfred. *Dictionnaire d'histoire et de géographie ecclésiastiques.* Paris: Letouzey et Ané, 1935.

Busa, Robert. *Index Thomisticus - Sancti Thomae Aquinatis Operum Omnium Indicus et Concordantiae.* 49 vol. Stuttgart-Bad Canstatt: Frommaun-Holzboog, 1974.

D'Alès, A. *Dictionnaire apologétique de la foi catholique.* Paris: Beauchesne, 1911.

Denzinger, H., and Schönmetzer, A. *Enchiridon Symbolorum - Definitionum et Decretionum de Rebus Fidei et Morum.* Herder, Friburgi Brisgoviae, 1963.

Lichtenberger, Frédéric. *Encyclopédie des sciences religieuses.* 13 vol. Paris: Fischbacher, 1882.

Vacant, A. et Mangnot, S. *Dictionnaire de Théologie catholique.* 30 vol. Paris: Letouzey et Ané, 1946.

Viller, M. *Dictionnaire de spiritualité, ascétique et mystique.* 14 vol. Paris: Beauchesne, parus 1992.

2. Catholicism and Protestantism

Arnaud, E. *Histoire des Protestants du Vivarais et du Velay Pays de Languedoc: de la Réforme à la Révolution*, Paris, Grassart, 1888.

Aquinas, Thomas. *Summa Theologica.* Roma, Marietti, 1948.

St. Augustine. *De cathechisandis rudibus,* XXVI.

Autin, Albert. *L'échec de la réforme en France au XVIe siècle.* Paris: Colin, 1918.

Baubérot, Jean. *Le protestantisme doit-il mourir?* Paris, Seuil, 1988.

_____. "Le Tricentenaire de la révocation de l'édit de Nantes." *Archives de Sciences Sociales des Religions*, octobre-décembre 1986, 62/2, p. 179-202.

Baud, Henri. *Le diocèse de Genève-Annecy.* Paris: Beauchesne, 1985.

Baum, G. et Cunitz, ed., *Histoire ecclésiastique des églises réformées au royaume de France.* 3 vol. Paris: Fischbacher, 1883.

Bergeal, Catherine et Durrleman, Antoine. *Protestantisme et liberté en France au 17e siècle, de l'Edit de Nantes à sa révocation, 1598-1685.* Carrières-sous-Poissy: La Cause, 1985.

Berkhof, Louis. *Reformed Dogmatics.* 3 vol. Grand Rapids: Eerdman, 1932.

Blet, Pierre, s.j. *Les assemblés du clergé et Louis XIV - de 1670 à 1693.* Roma, Universatà Gregoriana Editrice, 1972.

_____. *Histoire de la Représentation Diplomatique du Saint Siège des origines à l'aube du XIXe siècle.* Citta' del Vaticano, Archivio Vaticano, 1982.

Bornert, René. *La réforme protestante du culte à Strasbourg au XVI siècle (1523-1598).* Leiden: Brill, 1981.

Boussuet, Jacques Bénigne. *Histoire des Variations des eglises protestantes.* Paris: Desprez, 1691.

Courvoisier, Jacques. *De la réforme au protestantisme.* Paris: Beauchesne, 1977.

Daniel-Rops, H. *The Catholic Reformation.* New York: E. Dutton, 1962.

Davidson, N. S. *La contre réforme.* Paris: Cerf, 1989.

Dawson, Christopher. *The Dividing of Christendom.* New York: Sheed and Ward, 1965.

Desgraves, Louis. *Répertoire des ouvrages de controverse entre Catholiques et Protestants en France, 1598-1685.* 2 vol. Genève: Droz, 1984-1985.

Devos, R. et Brosperin, B. *La Savoie de la Réforme à la Révolution française.* Ouest-France: Rennes, 1985.

Devresse, R. *Théodore de Mopsueste. Homélies catéchétiques*, Città del Vaticano, Tonneau-Devresse, 1939.

Dolan, John. *History of the Reformation: A Conciliatory Assessment of Opposite Views.* New York: Desclée, 1965.

Dompnier, Bernard. *Le venin de l'hérésie (Image du protestantisme et combat catholique au XVIIe siècle).* Centurion, 1985.

Doney, Mgr. *Catéchisme du Concile de Trente.* 2 vol. Dijon: Lagier, 1844.

Dumeige, G. *La foi catholique.* Orante, Paris, 1961.

Elie, H. *Le traité de l'infini de Jean Mair.* Paris, 1938.

Farge, James. *Orthodoxy and Reform in Early Reformation France: The Faculty of Theology of Paris, 1500-1543.* Leiden: Brill, 1985.

Fouilloux, E. "L'oecuménisme d'avant-hier à aujourd'hui." *Les quatre fleuves*, no. 20, 1984.

Haag, Eugène et Emile. *La France protestante ou vie des protestants français qui se sont fait un nom dans l'histoire.* Genève: Slatkine Reprints, 1966, 10 vol.

Jedin, Hubert. *A History of the Council of Trent.* Vol. 1 & 2 (of 5). London, Paris: Nelson, 1961.

Kappler, Emile. *Conférences théologiques entre catholiques et protestants.* 1980.

Lebèque, Raymond. *La tragédie religieuse en France.* Paris: Champion, 1929.

Léonard, Emile G. *Histoire générale du Protestantisme.* Paris. 3 vol. PUF, 1961.

Maimbourg, Louis. *La méthode pacifique pour ramener sans dispute les protestants à la vraie foy sur le point de l'Eucharistie.* Paris, 1670.

Nugent, Donald. *Ecumenism in the Age of Reformation: the Colloquy of Poissy.* Cambridge, Mass: Harvard, 1974.

Romier, Lucien. *Catholiques et Huguenots à la cour de Charles IX.* Paris: Perrin, 1924.

Snoeks, Remi. *L'argument de tradition dans la controverse eucharistique entre catholiques et réformés français au XVIIe siècle.* Pub. Univ. Louvain, 1951.

Solé, Jacques. *Le débat entre protestants et catholiques français de 1598 à 1685.* Paris, Aux Amateurs de Livres, 1985.

Stauffenegger, Roger. *Eglise et société - Genève au XVIIe siècle.* Genève: Droz, 1984.

Strohl, Henry. *La pensée de la réforme.* Naufchatel: Delachaux et Niestlé, 1952.

Venard, M. *Réforme, Réformation, Préréforme. Contre Réforme...Etude de vocabulaire chez les historiens récents de langue française. Historiographie de la Réforme.* Paris: Delachaux et Niestlé, 1977.

Ward, A. W. and Prothero, G. W. *The Cambridge Modern History.* New York: The Macmillan Co., 1934.

3. Calvin

Cadier, Jean. *La doctrine calviniste de la sainte Cène.* Monpellier: Fac. Prot. de Théo. de Montpellier, 1951.

_____. "Une nouvelle contribution à la théologie de la sainte cène." *Etudes théologiques et religieuses*, 1956, no. 1, p. 36-45.

Dedieu, Joseph. "Calvin et Calviniste: la spiritualité calviniste." *Dictionnaire de spiritualité, ascétique et mystique.* II, col. 23-49.

Dominice, Max. *Calvin, homme d'Église.* Genève: Labor et Fides, 1971.

Ganoczy, Alexandre. *Calvin: Théologien de l'eglise et du ministère.* Paris: Cerf, 1964.

Imbart de la Tour. *Calvin et l'Institution chrétienne. Paris, 1935.*

McDonnell, Kilian. *John Calvin, the Church and the Eucharist.* Princeton, N.J.: Princeton Univ. Press, 1967.

McNeill, John T. *Calvin: Institutes of the Christian Religion.* 2 vols. Library of Christian Classics. Philadelphia: Westminster Press, 1960.

Niesel, Wilhelm. *The Theology of Calvin.* (tr. H. Knight) Philadelphia: Westminster Press, 1938.

114

Park, Gon Taik. *La doctrine de la sainte cène chez Calvin*. Montpellier: Thesis, 1984.

Prestwich, Menna. *International Calvinism: 1541-1715*. Oxford: Clarendon Press, 1985.

Quere, Ralph Walter. *Melanchthon's Christum Cognoscere: Christ's Efficacious Presence in the Eucharistic Theology of Melanchthon*. Nieuwkopp: B. de Graaf, 1977.

Reid, J. K. S. *Calvin: Theological Treatises*. Library of Christian Classics (V. XXII). Philadelphia: Westminster Press, 1964.

Schmidt, Albert-Marie, ed. *Epître à Sadolet, Trois Traités*. Paris: "Je Sers," 1934, p. 63.

Stauffer, R. *Dieu, la création et la Providence dans la prédication de Calvin*. Berne: 1978.

Wallace, Ronald S. *Calvin's Doctrine of the Word and Sacrament*. London: Oliver and Boyd, 1953.

Wendel, François. *Calvin (The Origins and Development of his Religious Thought)*. Translated by P. Mairet. New York: Harper and Row, 1950.

4. Francis de Sales

Bremond, Henri. *Histoire littéraire du sentiment religieux en France depuis la fin des guerres de religion jusqu'à nos jours*. Vol. II. Paris: Bloud et Gay, 1929-1936.

Ephraim, Frère et Dr. Mardon-Robinson. *Le chemin des nuages ou la folie de Dieu: de l'angoisse à la sainteté*. Nouan-le-Fuzelier: Ed. du Lion de Juda, 1988.

Gaberel, J. *La mission de Saint François de Sales en Savoie*. Genève: Gruaz, 1855.

Guillot, Alexandre. *François de Sales et les Protestants*. Genève: Taponnier, 1873.

Kleinman, Ruth. *Saint François de Sales and the Protestants*. Genève: Droz, 1962.

Lajeunie, Etienne-Marie. *Saint François de Sales. L'homme, la pensée, l'action*. Paris: Victor, 1966.

Lecestre, Léon. *Saint François de Sales*. Paris: Henri Laurens, 1934.

Leroux, Jean-Luc. *L'Eucharistie dans la théologie salésienne*. Lyon: Thesis, 1977.

Lomoro, Henrichette. *Attualità ecclesiologica de San Francesco di Sales; Les "Controverses" et la "Lumen Gentium."* Milano: Instituto Propaganda Libraria, 1976.

Marceau, William. *L'optimisme dans les oeuvres de Saint François de Sales*. Paris: Lethielleux, 1973.

Marsollier, M. *La vie de Saint François de Sales: évêque et prince de Genève et instituteur de l'ordre de la Visitation de Sainte Marie*. 2 vol. Paris, 1757.

Perate, André. *La mission de François de Sales dans le Chablais*. Rome: Documents inédits tirés des archives du Vatican, 1886.

Piccard, Louis-Etienne. *La mission de Saint François de Sales en Chablais*. Thonon-les-Bains: Pellissier, 1932.

Ravier, André. *Francis de Sales - Sage and Saint*. San Francisco: Ignatius Press, 1988.

Salesius, Franciscus. *Discorso di sagre controversis de s. F. di S. aisigg. del Magistrato della città di Tonone della religione pretesa riformata: posti in luce le prima volta dall' originaria lor lingua franzese nel italiano dall'ab. Agostino Maria Taja....* 260 pp. Roma: Barnabo, 1710.

Tournade, Michel. *La nature dans l'oeuvre de François de Sales*, Thesis, Lille: A.N.R.T., 1989.

5. Théodore de Bèze

Anderson, Marvin W. "Theodore Beza - Savant or Scholastic." *Theologische Zeitschrift*, 1978/4, p. 320-332.

Baird, Henry-Martyn. *Théodore Bèze, the Counsellor of the French Reformation*. New York: Putnam, 1899.

Bayle, Pierre. *Dictionnaire historique et critique*. Vol. I, p. 796-810. Amsterdam, 1734.

Bèze, Théodore de. "La confession de foi du chrétien." Trad. de M. Reveillaud, *La revue réformée*, Tome VI, No. 24, 1954/5, p. 68-88.

Bolsec, J. H. *Vies de Jean Calvin et de Théodore de Bèze*. Genève: Vignier, 1835.

Dufour, Alain. *Le colloque de Poissy: Mélanges d'histoire du XVIe siècle offerts à Henry Meylan*. Genève, 1970.

116

Dufour, A. et Nicollier, B. *Correspondance de Théodore be Bèze*: recueillie par Hippolyte Aubert, Société du Musée Historique de la Réformation. Genève: Librairie Droz, 1960.

Emery, Pierre-Yves. *Le sacrifice eucharistique selon les théologiens réformés français du XVIIe siècle*. Delachaux et Niestlé, 1959.

Fatio, Olivier. *Théodore d Bèze ou les débuts de l'orthodoxie réformée*. *Hokhma*, No. 28, 1985, p. 1-24.

Foxen, Davis. *The Dogmatic Interpretation of Sacramental Character According to the Discussions and Documents of the Council of Trent.* Gregorian. Thesis. 1975.

Gardy, Frédéric. *Bibliographie des oeuvres théologiques, littéraires, historiques et juridiques de Théodore de Bèze*. Genève: Droz, 1960.

Geisendorf, Paul-F. *Théodore de Bèze*. Genève: Jullien, 1967.

Goosen, Werner. *Les origines de l'Eucharistie, sacrement et sacrifice*. Paris: Gembloux, 1931.

Gy, Pierre-Marie. "L'eucharistie dans la tradition de la prière et de la doctrine." *La Maison-Dieu*, 137, p. 81-102.

Hamon, Léon. *Un siècle et demi d'histoire protestante: Théodore de Bèze et les Protestants sujets du roi*. Paris: Edition de la Maison, 1989.

Hotibert, Pierre-Marie. *La formule "ex opere operato" chez Saint Thomas.* Notes de cours. Paris: Inst. catholique, 1989, p. 1-13.

Journet, Charles. *Le mystère de l'eucharistie*. Paris: Tequi, 1981.

Jungmann, Joseph-André. *Missarum Sollemnia (explication de la Messe romaine)*. Paris: Aubier, 1953.

Kickel, Walter. *Vernunft und Offenbarung bei Theodor Beza: zum Problem des Verhaltnisses von Theologie, Philosophie und Statt*. Neukirchen-Vluyn: Neukirchener Verlag des Erziehungsvereins, 1967.

Klipffel, D. Henri. *Le colloque de Poissy. Etude sur la crise religieuse et politique de 1561*. Paris: Librarie Internationale, 1867.

Leenhardt, Franz - J. *Le sacrement de la Sainte Cène*, Paris: Delachaux et Niestlé, 1941.

Leger, Raymond. *Le concept de présence réele dans l'eucharistie d'après Saint Thomas et ses principaux commentateurs*. Paris. Thesis. 1960.

Letham, Robert. "Theodore Beza: A Reassesssment." *Scottish Journal of Theology*. 1987, Vol. 40, pp. 25-40.

Lubac, Henri de. *Méditation sur l'église*. Paris Aubier, 1953 (2nd ed.).

Martelet, Gustave. *Résurrection, eucharistie et genèse de l'homme*. Paris: Desclée, 1972.

Martins, José Saraiva. *The Sacrament of the New Alliance*. Pontifical Urban University (Rome), Bangalore, 1988.

Meylan, Henri. *D'Erasme à Théodore de Bèze. Problèmes de l'Eglise et de l'Ecole chez les Réformes*. Genève: Droz, 1976.

Miyakawa, Toshiyuki. *The ecclesiastical meaning of the "res et sacramentum": the visible Church as the effect of the Sacraments*. Paris. Thesis. 1968.

Motte, A. -R. "La chronologie relative du quodl. VII et du commentaire sur le IVe livre des Sentences." *Notes et communications*, No. 2. avril, 1931, p. 29-37.

Nau, Paul. *Le mystère du Corps et du Sang du Seigneur*. Solesmes, Aubin, 1976.

Neuner, J. and Dupuis, J. *The Christian Faith in the Doctrinal Documents of the Catholic Church*. New York: Alba House, 1981.

Puaux, Franck. "Théodore de Bèze et Saint François de Sales." *Revue Chrétienne*, Paris, 1894, pp. 168-176.

Raitt, Jill. *The Eucharistic Theology of Theodore Beza: Development of the Reformed Doctrine*. American Academy of Studies in Religion, No. 4. Atlanta, Ga.: Scholars Press, 1976.

Reveillaud, Michel. *"La Confession de foi du chrétien."* *La revue réformée*, Nos. 23-24, 1955, pp. 1-100.

Scheeben, M-J. *Les mystères du christianisme*. Bruges: Desclée de Brouwer, 1959.

Schillebeeckx, E. *La présence du Christ dans l'eucharistie*. Paris: Cerf, 1970.

Thurian, Max. *L'eucharistie, Mémorial du Seigneur*. Paris: Niestlé, 1959.

Tillard, J.-M. *L'eucharistie: Pâque de l'Eglise*. Paris: Cerf, 1964.

Zahrnt, Heinz. *Dans l'attente de Dieu - l'Eglise avant la Réformation*. Paris: Casterman, 1970.

Zizioulas, Jean. *L'eucharistie*. Paris: Mame, 1970.

INDEX

Substance, 6, 7, 8, 9, 10, 16, 18, 19,
20, 22, 23, 36, 47, 51, 52, 53,
60, 61, 63, 73, 90, 95, 100,
102, 105
Summa, 27, 28, 80, 91, 97, 105, 111
Superstition, 4

T

Theologian, 23, 31, 35, 40, 69, 74,
79, 94, 99
Thomas, 4, 23, 27, 28, 53, 69, 85,
87, 89, 90, 98, 105, 111, 116
Tournon, 74, 75, 77
Tradition, 2, 32, 35, 40, 41, 48, 50,
54, 63, 65, 83, 89, 113, 116
Traité, 2, 3, 4, 21, 25, 26, 32, 37,
91, 109, 112, 114
Transubstantiation, 4, 16, 17, 37,
73, 84, 93, 96, 97, 98, 99, 100,
102, 103, 104, 105
Treatise, 3, 14, 21, 36, 37, 38, 87,
101, 108, 114
Trent, 1, 4, 28, 29, 36, 41, 50, 63,
65, 67, 78, 79, 81, 84, 85, 89,
90, 92, 96, 98, 105, 107, 112,
116
Trinity, 32, 104

W

William of Ockham, 68

Z

Zwingli, 17, 22

TORONTO STUDIES IN THEOLOGY

23. Eric Voegelin, **Political Religions,** T. J. DiNapoli and E. S. Easterly III (trans.)

24. Rolf Ahlers, **The Barmen Theological Declaration of 1934: The Archeology of a Confessional Text**

25. Kenneth Cauthen, **Systematic Theology: A Modern Protestant Approach**

26. Hubert G. Locke (ed.), **The Barmen Confession: Papers from the Seattle Assembly**

27. Barry Cooper, **The Political Theory of Eric Voegelin**

28. M. Darrol Bryant and Hans R. Huessy (eds.), **Eugen Rosenstock-Huessy: Studies in His Life and Thought**

29. John Courtney Murray, **Matthias Scheeben on Faith: The Doctoral Dissertation of John Courtney Murray,** D. Thomas Hughson (ed.)

30. William J. Peck (ed.), **New Studies in Bonhoeffer's** Ethics

31. Robert B. Sheard, **Interreligious Dialogue in the Catholic Church Since Vatican II: An Historical and Theological Study**

32. Paul Merkley, **The Greek and Hebrew Origins of Our Idea of History**

33. F. Burton Nelson (ed.), **The Holocaust and the German Church Struggle: A Search for New Directions**

34. Joyce A. Little, **Toward a Thomist Methodology**

35. Dan Cohn-Sherbok, **Jewish Petitionary Prayer: A Theological Exploration**

36. C. Don Keyes, **Foundations For an Ethic of Dignity: A Study in the Degradation of the Good**

37. Paul Tillich, **The Encounter of Religions and Quasi-Religions: A Dialogue and Lectures,** Terence Thomas (ed.)

38. Arnold A. van Ruler, **Calvinist Trinitarianism and Theocentric Politics: Essays Toward a Public Theology,** John Bolt (trans.)

39. Julian Casserley, **Evil and Evolutionary Eschatology: Two Essays,** C. Don Keyes (ed.)

40. J. M. B. Crawford and J. F. Quinn , **The Christian Foundations of Criminal Responsibility: A Philosophical Study of Legal Reasoning**

41. William C. Marceau, **Optimism in the Works of St. Francis De Sales**

42. A. James Reimer, **The Emanuel Hirsch and Paul Tillich Debate: A Study in the Political Ramifications of Theology**

43. George Grant, et al., Two Theological Languages **by George Grant and Other Essays in Honour of His Work,** Wayne Whillier (ed.)

44. William C. Marceau, **Stoicism and St. Francis De Sales**

45. Lise van der Molen, **A Complete Bibliography of the Writings of Eugen Rosenstock-Huessy**

46. Franklin H. Littell (ed.), **A Half Century of Religious Dialogue, 1939-1989: Making the Circles Larger**